To: Bill and Mary Hunt
Best wishes
Lawrence Small
April 20, 1995

Journey with the Law

The Life of Judge William J. Jameson

by Lawrence F. Small

Best Wishes
Lawrence F. Small

Published by Rocky Mountain College

Library of Congress Catalog Card Number: 84-61724
ISBN 0-934318-44-1

Publishing Consultant: Falcon Press Publishing Co., Inc.,
Helena, and Billings, Montana

Painting by James M. Haughey, Retirement Dinner, 1969

DEDICATION

For Bill and Mildred, whose journey together with the law is an inspiration for the many who have known them.

We have always been prone to self-criticism. Certainly no thoughtful person would wish to mute the debate and dissent which have strengthened our democracy. No traditions are more firmly rooted, or more essential to the ultimate preservation of our liberties, than the rights of speech, press and assembly.

One might wish, however, for a better balance and a higher level of responsibility in the criticism. America, its institutions and the value of our people, deserve a better billing than they often receive. In our concern with the present and our serious social problems, we are losing a proper perspective of history. History balances the frustrations of 'how far we have to go' with the satisfaction of 'how far we have come.' It teaches us tolerance for the human shortcomings and imperfections which are not uniquely of our generation, but of all time.

It would be irrational to say that all of the criticisms of America and its institutions are unfounded. Yet excessive self-flagellation is destroying the ties that bind us together. We as a people, are entitled to recall that the history of America is a proud and decent one. However slow and painful progress at times may seem, the consistent vision is of a society in which all can live in self-respect and responsibly pursue their own aspirations.

— *Lewis F. Powell*
Associate Justice
U.S. Supreme Court

Justice, Sir, is the greatest interest of man here on Earth.

— *Daniel Webster*

The Spirit of Liberty is the spirit which is not too sure it is right.

— *Judge Learned Hand*

I enjoy my work. I love the law.

— *Judge William J. Jameson*

TABLE OF CONTENTS

FOREWORD

I am glad that this book was written. It describes the life of Bill Jameson from his birth through his presidency of the American Bar Association and his subsequent service on the federal bench. This book reveals the roots of Bill's faith and of his desire for scholarship. It pictures a man independent in his own thinking but deeply aware of his responsibilities to his family, his community, and his country. It shows Bill as a boy, a teen-ager, and an adult, pursuing excellence in his studies, in his work, and in his relationships with those around him. *Sub silentio* the author explains why Bill Jameson is a modest man—why there is no need in him, secure in the knowledge of his own diligence and capabilities, to be anything other than himself.

One who writes a foreword to a book should not write a book, and for that reason I must capsulize the eminence of Bill Jameson as a judge. I have heard the voice of the lawyers—those who won before Judge Jameson and agree with his rulings, those who lost and perhaps do not—and in that voice there is consensus as to the gentleness, the even temper, and the genuine care that Jameson, the judge, has exhibited in the courtroom. There is consensus that he has exercised the power of reason rather than the power of authority.

The esteem in which Judge Jameson is held by his fellow judges stems not so much from his demeanor as from the intelligence and unremitting diligence with which he does his homework. That homework consists of distilling the truth from the evidence in the case, much of which is partisan and much of which is contradictory; it consists in hours of searching through the hundreds of books in his library for the statutes, administrative rulings, and decisions which bear upon the subject, and then interpreting, or perhaps synthesizing, the statutes and decisions to find a rule truly applicable. There are no headlines in this kind of searching, but the quality of Judge Jameson's homework has not gone unnoticed by his colleagues on the bench. I have heard the voice of judges from Maine to California and from Washington to Florida, and the voice speaks of Judge Jameson's careful, knowledgeable, and scholarly opinions. This consensus is evidenced by the many invitations which have been extended to Judge Jameson to sit with courts of appeals in many circuits, including the Temporary Emergency Court of Appeals, and in the numerous appointments he has received to serve on judicial committees.

Some years ago, at a dinner given in honor of Judge Jameson, I expressed the idea that, if in some critical moment my country needed to personify American justice, Judge Jameson would meet every qualification.

This book describes the forces that moulded the character that enabled Bill Jameson, the man, to become not only a judge, but the kind of judge he is.

Russell E. Smith
U.S. Senior District
Judge

INTRODUCTION

It was about 1968 that my acquaintance began with Judge Jameson. He had become a Trustee of Rocky Mountain College, where I had been serving in the presidency since 1965. The times were stressful in higher education, with demonstrations, office take-overs, violence on some large campuses, and a growing distrust and distance between town and gown. While Rocky Mountain was in the backstream of protest, some of the winds of change were being felt in such issues as co-ed residence halls, relaxed drinking regulations, and a larger role for faculty and students in the governance of the institution. I shall always be grateful for the Judge's quiet advocacy of the "balanced perspective" within the counsels of the Board.

After I returned to the classroom in 1975, I (and my students) had the pleasure of annual visits, with the Judge lecturing on the American court system or sharing his reflections on a half-century of Montana law and politics. It was in the latter that the thought came of a book about one of the truly notable careers in the history of our state. Later, while working with Judge Jameson on *A Century of Politics on the Yellowstone*, I obtained his permission to undertake the project. I want to thank him here for the full cooperation, without which this work would not have been possible.

One day his wife, Mildred, said to me, her eyes alight with merriment, "Don't make him sound too good. I won't be able to live with him." No one knew better than she how free he is of pretentiousness. His engrained modesty, she had noted in a letter to his sister, Lucille, was one of the reasons why he was so widely admired within the organized Bar. The high esteem had been expressed by many, but nowhere more succinctly than by President Robert W. Meserve on a particularly memorable occasion: "It is said that the law is a public profession. The tradition of service and leadership which supports that profession is nowhere better illustrated than in the career of Judge William J. Jameson. He is without peer in his dedication to his community, his native state of Montana, the organized bar and, above all, to the unending search for justice itself. He has brought honor to his profession and it is fitting that he be honored with the American Bar Association Medal, the Association's highest award."

In a very real way, this book is a shared effort to celebrate a distinguished Montanan and his wife. I am indebted to Rocky Mountain College for reduced teaching responsibilities during the spring semester of this year, and for a research grant, without which the project could not have been completed at this time. Dr. Bruce T. Alton, President, and Dr. R. Dean Boswell, Jr., Academic Vice President and Dean of the College, have been supportive and a source of encouragement. I wish to acknowledge with appreciation financial assistance provided by the law firm of Crowley, Haughey, Hanson, Toole & Dietrich. Parmly Billings Library and Linda Weirather, Coordinator of Public Services, have been helpful in making available microfilm and other research data.

Judge Jameson's cooperation has been invaluable, not only in granting several interviews and placing at my disposal extensive materials, but in reading the text and making constructive suggestions. Similarly, his sister, Lucille, has made a major contribution with her written recollections of early family history, her carefully kept scrapbooks on the Judge's career, and in reading and making suggestions on the text. Others who have helped in examining the manuscript are Mary Honaker and U.S. Senior District Judge Russell E. Smith. I would also like to acknowledge the help of Thelma L. Green, the Judge's secretary, my son, Daniel for his work on the Index, and Jens Selvig for reproducing the photographs. The project has remained on schedule thanks to the

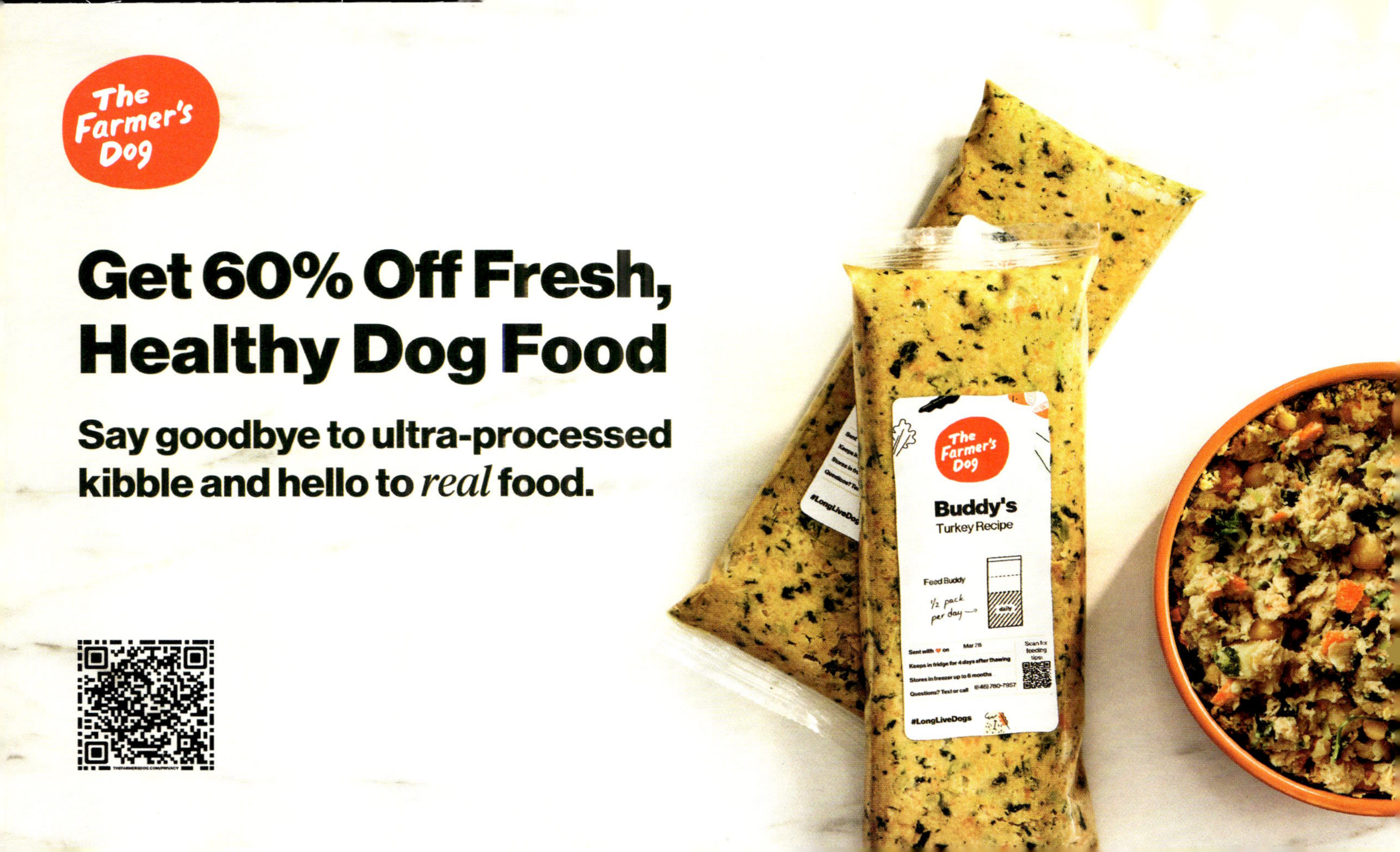
The Farmer's Dog
Get 60% Off Fresh,
Healthy Dog Food
Say goodbye to ultra-processed
kibble and hello to real food.
THEFARMERSDOG.COM/PRIVACY
The Farmer's Dog
Buddy's
Turkey Recipe
Feed Buddy
½ pack per day
daily
Sent with ♥ on Mar 28
Keeps in fridge for 4 days after thawing
Stores in freezer up to 6 months
Questions? Text or call (646) 780-7957
Scan for feeding tips:
#LongLiveDogs

good efforts of Dr. Dale Zimdars and son David who prepared the manuscript for telecommunication and of Falcon Press Publishing Company, the publishing consultants. Finally, my wife, Elfie, has provided that kind of support and encouragement that this writer needed to get the job done.

Lawrence F. Small
Summer, 1984

PROLOGUE

The country lawyer, as he called himself, looked out over the crowded Imperial Ballroom of the Hotel Statler in Boston. It was August 27, 1953 and the American Bar Association was holding its Diamond Jubilee Meeting. That made it one of the most notable in the seventy-seven year history of the Association, but in addition this meeting was being viewed as the beginning of a new era, in which the A.B.A. would devote less attention to strictly professional concerns and more of its energies to broad questions of public policy.

Most of the 4000 delegates seemed ready for the change, but meanwhile they had been treating themselves to the sights, sounds, and savors of historic Boston. As *Life* for September 7 would observe:"they brought an atmosphere of decorum rare in convention cities as they went about sampling the local sea food, visiting law libraries, touring the land marks of the American Revolution, which members of their profession are given so much credit for starting."

Seated near incoming president William J. Jameson of Billings, Montana was Chief Justice Frederick M. Vinson, who would introduce the speaker for this fourth session, The Right Honorable Lord Simonds, The Lord High Chancellor of Great Britain. Vinson joked with Jameson about the "country lawyer" business and John

W. Davis, a past president of the A.B.A. and Democratic nominee for the presidency in 1924, joined in. Vinson recalled his obscure beginnings in Louisa, Kentucky, while Davis noted his humble origins in Clarksburg, West Virginia. Both doubted that Jameson's home town, then in the throes of an oil boom and growing by leaps and bounds, justified his claim. But, then, there was no doubt that Montana was rather removed from the vital center of Association affairs.

Actually, the Treasure State was the 32nd to provide a president for the A.B.A. While its leaders had been drawn from all sections of the country, the metropolitan areas had been best represented, with sixteen of the seventy-seven coming from New York City, five from Chicago, and four from Philadelphia. Few, however, had had a longer term of service in the Association and had been more faithful to their duties than the lawyer from Billings.

Hardly had he been admitted to the Montana Bar in 1922 than he was serving as its secretary, gaining friends and winning the respect of his colleagues that would bring him the presidency in 1936. He had joined the A.B.A. ten years earlier. He had been a member of the House of Delegates since its inception in 1936 and had never missed a meeting! He had served on the Board of Governors, as an Assembly Delegate, and on various committees, reflecting assignments of increasing responsibility within the Association. It had meant over the years many meetings and numerous trips away from home, but it was an important part of a life-long ambition.

From childhood he had known that he wanted to be a lawyer. As a sixth-grader in the little mining community of Roundup, he watched for the visiting judge from Billings or Lewistown to hold court in town. Whether or not his attorney father was involved in a case, young "Willie" was often an interested spectator. By the time he was a high school junior, his thoughts on the legal profession had found a focus in an English theme which received an A+ and his teacher's comment: "The best thing you have written."

That was a distant yesterday. Yet what he had written with the enthusiasm and notable clarity of youth about the practice of the law—the need for diligent study of the statutes, integrity in the face of many temptations, courage to bear the disappointments, humility and humanitarian caring to keep first things first—these had become the compass points of his career.

The road to Boston, he reflected, had been traveled in the invaluable company of family and friends, without whose support and encouragement this high moment in his life and career would hardly have been possible. Courage he had learned from his father, who had read law as a Butte miner, determined to make his way into the profession. What satisfaction the elder Jameson found in seeing his son receive full legal training at the law school in Missoula! Mother and sister Lucille had never ceased to nurture his hopes. Through the years Lucille had followed his career with more than usual sisterly interest, as evidenced by her carefully kept scrapbooks.

But one, beyond all others, had shared so fully the burdens and the rewards of his chosen work and his deepening involvement in the American Bar Association. For thirty years, Mildred had been the understanding and sympathetic wife, so much a part of this moment in Boston. Unfortunately, she would not be with him during much of the strenuous year ahead. Soon she would be going to Rochester for serious surgery and a long period of convalescence. But she would know his day-by-day itinerary and would be with him in spirit as he crisscrossed the country, fulfilling the demands of a very busy schedule.

So, seated amidst the leaders of the legal profession in the land, the incoming president could reflect upon the meeting of two ways—that which reached back from this moment to his Montana childhood and the way of a future full of service to the profession he enjoyed so much.

CHAPTER ONE

HERITAGE

It was from the rolling, green hills of Northern Ireland that the Jamesons (or Jamisons) had made their way to the new world. Once their people had lived in Scotland, before the English government had transplanted them across the Irish Sea. The hard-working, Presbyterian Scots were to live among the unruly Irish Catholics and help to bring peace and industry to the northern counties. They did their job all too efficiently and were soon competing with English landlords and manufacturers. The inevitable restrictions fell upon them in one act of Parliament after another, until by the early 1700's they were in such want that many sought escape to the new world.

Many came as indentured servants, penniless and binding their labor for a chance to begin again. Others sought the isolation of the interior to squat upon the land. In western Pennsylvania and the backcountry of the South, the Scotch-Irish mingled with other nationalities and produced a hardy new breed of American equal to the ordeal of frontier living. They raised large families, while more and more of their kindred came across the Atlantic, until they numbered 300,000 by the eve of the Revolution.

The Jamisons (as the name was first spelled) settled in eastern Pennsylvania, where one William Jamison bore the name that would be carried through several generations. Little is known of

William Jamison, Grandfather of Judge Jameson

him or the time of his coming to the new world, but it may have been his son or grandson, Joseph, who married Mary Rough of Stockertown in the 1830's. Of that union another William Jamison was born in Tomagrea, Schuylkill County in 1838, one of eight children. Notable was the defection of a sister, who broke the ranks of devout Presbyterianism and became the family outcast when she wed an Irish Catholic and embraced his faith. But time would mostly heal the wounds and was helped when her daughter married the son of a Presbyterian preacher.[1]

With the coming of the Civil War, William signed on for the stipulated three months (at that time) with the Pennsylvania Volunteers. Later, he served with the 4th Army Corps at Nashville, Tennessee. His final enlistment was on February 11, 1864 for another year. He was captured by the Confederates and sat out the rest of the war in Libby Prison. A one-time tobacco warehouse in Richmond, Virginia, it was second only to Andersonville in Georgia as the most notorious of the Confederate prisons. Food was scarce and bad, and sanitation facilities were virtually nonexistent. William was among the thousands who did not survive. Chronic diarrhea undermined his health. He did live to see the war over and was on his way home aboard the steamer *Commonwealth* when he died and was buried at a military post.

Wife Rebecca first heard the sad news as she waited for her husband at the railroad station. As she fainted, one of the family grabbed infant son William James, while another eased her fall. Her family, the Williamses, had come from around Cardiff in the rich coal mining region of South Wales. Cardiff, in fact, had become one of the leading coal-shipping ports in the world, but the transition in the early years of the nineteenth century from pastoral and agricultural ways to industrialization brought serious unrest and growing numbers of Welshmen seeking the new world. She was three when her family uprooted and came to Olyphant, north of Scranton, to work in Pennsylvania's coal fields. There she had grown to womanhood as the oldest in a family of six.

Rebecca's widow's pension was hardly enough to support her and the baby, so she lived with her husband's parents for a while, learning the fine art of "Pennsylvania Dutch" cooking. Little did she realize that her culinary accomplishments would be utilized later in operating a boarding-house on the Montana frontier. The attractive young widow had several suitors and eventually married a coal miner named George Bennett. Four children would join little William James Jamison in the family.

Some time prior to 1880, Bennett decided that Nevada's silver mines had more to offer than the coal fields of Pennsylvania. The immense riches of the Comstock Lode in the Virginia Range, discovered in 1859, had helped sustain Union credit during the war and had produced several "silver kings" like George Hearst. But by the 1870's the Comstock was in decline. So was the price of the precious metal, due to increased production by Nevada's and Colorado's mines. Mining interests succeeded in having silver monetized again through the Bland-Allison Act of 1878, but the government purchased only the minimum amount required by law ($2 million a month at the market price). The commercial price of silver continued to sag badly, until it reached a ratio of 20:1 to gold by 1890. So Nevada was hardly the place of Bennett's expectations.

Yet he and his family made lasting friendships during their stay at Tuscarora, in the mountains of that name in northern Nevada. Years later they would be recalling happy memories of their time there. By 1883, however, Bennett was ready to join the growing migration of miners to a new El Dorado called Butte City, perched high in the mountains of southwestern Montana Territory.

Butte City had first been a gold camp, with placer mining beginning on Silver Bow Creek in the summer of 1864. By 1868, however, the surface deposits were playing out and miners were moving on. Seasoned argonauts surmised that there was vast mineral wealth beneath their feet, but they lacked the technology to get at it. So Butte began to die, like countless other places on the mining frontier. Early day resident George P. Porter recalled that there were few left by 1874, perhaps 50 or so persistent ones occupying a score of houses, along with a school (6 pupils), a saloon, and a boarding house. He also fondly remembered that there were fish in the stream running through Yankee Doodle Gulch and strawberry bushes and flowers lining Silver Bow Creek. Trees and grass and flowers were in abundance; in fact, Butte was an alpine "jewel" without compare in the entire territory.[2]

Just when it seemed that the place was fated to become another ghost town, a tough breed of investors moved in with the mining know-how, the necessary resources, and the business acumen to pry open the mineral wealth of the "richest hill on earth." Their names would become near-legendary in the annals of the Treasure State—William L. Farlin, William Andrews Clark, Andrew Jackson Davis, Marcus Daly and the others. Silver mining came first and by 1876 Butte City was booming. It was incorporated with that name at a special session of the legislature in 1879 and then was designated the county seat when Silver Bow was separated from Deer Lodge County in 1881.

By 1883, when the Bennetts arrived, Butte City had also acquired a reputation for wild ways. Journalists and lecturers found a popular subject in picturing Butte as "the wickedest city of the West." The *Montana Standard* recalled: "Slandering of Butte had become a sort of a profession as far back as 1887." [3] The rough restlessness of the mining camp did live on in the feverish pace of city life. The general commotion of the place never seemed to lessen. There appeared to be no time for rest. For Lemuel Eli Quigg, feature writer for the *New York Tribune*, Butte's main folly was that people seemed possessed with working themselves to death. "You must keep going as the crowd goes," he wrote in July of 1889. "You can't lag behind while those around you, competing with you, are hurling themselves forward." In fact, Quigg concluded, one "does as much living in 10 years in Butte as in 20 years in the east." [4]

The town was tough and made little effort to conceal it. That also impressed Quigg, that Butte preferred candor to hypocrisy. There were no "side doors" or alley entrances for special patrons; rather, the "sun is permitted to shine through the clear glass windows upon the unjust as well as the just." The gambling houses operated with doors wide open, "without even as much as a wicker screen to shield their careless players." Butte was Butte and some years later, in 1903, Mayor Pat Mullins insisted on taking a touring President Teddy Roosevelt through the red light district, noting that it was "the finest sporting row in our country!"

But there were also seven churches in the overgrown mining camp by 1889 and Quigg could add: "the people of Butte are proud of everything they possess . . . their mines, . . . their stores, . . . their clubs, . . . their beer halls, and . . . their churches." Sunday was the busiest and noisiest day of the week, with citizens working and playing to the hilt, but apparently the clergy were not discouraged. The local press reported that "our churches are all running full blast." In addition to the Roman Catholic and mainline Protestant congregations, a People's Tabernacle was holding forth at the corner of Quartz and Wyoming Streets.

Fueling the frenetic pace of the town was the discovery of the rich copper deposits. By 1883 Marcus Daly and partners were ready to erect a massive copper reduction works and smelter 26 miles to the west, around which would arise the company town of Anaconda. Aside from the Anaconda mine, according to Reno Sales' count (*Underground Warfare At Butte*), there were at least 25 mining companies digging into the "hill." So Bennett had arrived at a propitious time when Butte was about to bound ahead. Unfortunately, his days were numbered. In the fall of 1885, just after completing a two-story house on Wyoming Street, he died unexpectedly. William Jamison, or Will, as his family called him, now 20, recorded in his diary: "Father died suddenly last Saturday, Sept. 26 and was buried Sunday by the I.O.O.F." Widowed once more, Rebecca took in boarders to make both ends meet.

II.

Will worked in the mines and turned over his wages of $3.00 a day to his mother. But from the entries in his diary, it is clear that he did not intend to spend his future underground in Butte. Somewhere along the way from his Scranton childhood, he had

Will Jameson

acquired a keen interest in learning and an ambition to make the most of his life. So there was $10 spent on a ten-week shorthand course and numerous lesser amounts on books for his library. He obtained Homer's *Iliad* for $1 and Green's *Making of England* for 20 cents. He was "much disappointed that the edition he ordered of Longfellow's poems did not contain 'Evangeline,' 'Hiawatha,' or 'Miles Standish'." From a friend he learned about the Chautauqua program and purchased course materials and other literature. That experiment in adult education, born on the shores of Lake Chautauqua in New York in 1874, featuring public lectures and courses of home study, proved to be such a success across the country that the courses were enrolling 100,000 people annually by the early 1890's. Will noted in his diary: "Am making good progress in the Chautauqua course, but not so good as I could wish. I will have to make review from time to time until I thoroughly understand all the studies." [5]

When the Presbyterian minister called, he congratulated Will upon having a taste for good books and invited him to the manse to see his library. Apparently, the good reverend depended upon book sales to augment his meager salary, for he unloaded on young Jamison eight volumes of *Johnson's Universal Cyclopedia* for the handsome sum of $56. Will had enough saved for three books and purchased the rest on installments. The set would provide excellent reference material for Jamison and his children in years to come.

Meanwhile, that fall of 1885 proved to be a difficult one for the family. Following the father's death in September, daughter Maryann came down with mountain typhoid fever and soon Will had it too. Miners were accustomed to helping when times turned hard, and in November they took a collection for the family which totaled over $453, enough to pay off the remaining debt on the house. Jamison recorded in his diary that he "got out for the first time since Oct. 26 on the 16 of December." Despite all the hardship, he noted that the family "passed a quiet, pleasant Christmas." Somehow he had saved enough money to buy earrings for his mother and books for his sisters and brother. His presents included Tennyson's and Browning's poems.

It took some time to regain his strength and get back into the mining routine. Work was not all that regular, with cave-ins, strikes, and fluctuating market conditions for silver and copper. Copper was a particular problem, with the long-established mining interests of Michigan resisting Butte's advancement into the copper market. Increased production from Montana and Arizona had already helped prices to fall to 14 cents a pound by 1884, but the Michigan-Boston magnates moved to depress prices further to drive the western competition out of business. By early 1886 copper had fallen to 10 cents a pound. Smaller Butte operations were forced to shut down and then Anaconda followed in August. Jamison noted in his diary for August 26, 1886: "silver & copper way down. Anaconda works, four or five mines in all closed down a few days ago. Outlook rather blue at present."

When employment was available, Will worked at the Parrot in various jobs, night-watching, car running, and as fireman, and hoped to become a stationary engineer. That would mean an increase of a dollar a day. Aside from his work and books, he indulged on occasion in the cultural life of the mining town. Butte was on the main line of the touring theater companies, attracting prominent actors, along with nationally famous minstrels and some notable prima donnas. For local talent there was the Butte Amateur Opera Company. Will noted in his diary seeing a road show called "May Blossom." "Money spent for such a healthy entertainment," he reasoned, "is well spent—provided you can afford it." He was less impressed with Miss Anna Eva Fay's spiritualistic performance at the theater, concluding that it was the greatest "bilk" that he had ever seen.

Transcending lesser events were three particular occasions which, more or less, engulfed the town. All Butte, Will observed, turned out for the Annual Miners' Day Parade each June, even when heavy rains meant wading ankle-deep in the mud. That happened in both 1885 and 1886, but nobody in the processions seemed to care. St. Patrick's Day tokened the dominant role of the Irish in the "melting pot" of immigrant nationalities that was Butte. Everywhere one saw the green—neckties for the men, ribbons and shamrocks for the ladies, even green collars for the dogs and horses, while bands played stirring Irish airs, speakers orated on the common destiny of America and Ireland, and the day was capped by lively dances at such places as the Miners Union and Hibernia Halls. A third event, of course, was the big Fourth of July celebration which was observed with notable enthusiasm throughout Montana Territory.[6]

About this time Will adopted the spelling of Jameson, and also began talking about ranching on the Flathead. It seemed an attractive option to all of the uncertainty surrounding mining, and he and a friend began giving it serious consideration. He hoped that he might also interest a relative with money in the venture; however, Rebecca was not impressed with his plans and the project died on the vine. "Mother has given up all idea of going on a ranch, so my scheme of going to Flathead will have to be abandoned." Her boarding house business was showing promise, despite the constant coming and going, due to work stoppages, talk of pay reduction, and the general migratory ways of many miners. Restless spirits talked with Will about looking in at Virginia City or going further afield to places like Salt Lake. At times Rebecca had as many as ten boarders and had to add a kitchen and wash room to meet the needs of the busy household.

Visitors at Wyoming Street included old friends from Tuscarora days and an occasional relative. Cousin Tommy Jamison, from Colorado, was an especially foot-loose one, who stopped in Butte long enough to "nick" Will for some travelling money. Young Jameson pondered in his diary his cousin's "rather wild" ways and was doubtless glad to help him along.

The election of 1886 found Will as a keenly interested observer, from a Republican viewpoint. He would not be tempted by a career in politics, though he would later serve as Public Administrator for Silver Bow County and then as City Attorney in Roundup. "Politics," he observed, "are booming this year." In the race for territorial delegate, the Democrats had renominated Joseph K. Toole, while the Republicans had turned once more to party stalwart Wilbur F. Sanders. Both candidates, in Jameson's view, had serious liabilities. Toole was saddled with " Cleveland's blunders," which he did not identify but might well have been referring to the President's stout opposition to the lumber companies' assault on the national forests and the stockmen's fencing of the public domain. The enviromentally-conscious Cleveland had summoned offending timber interests into court and had ordered all of the barbwire pulled up. Such actions riled westerners in both parties. As for Sanders, the one-time vigilante's candidacy was badly flawed by his railroad connections.

The campaign turned into a "lively and somewhat bitter fight," Jameson recorded in his diary.For the *Billings Daily Gazette*, the election was "the most bitterly contested . . . ever held in the territory."[7] Toole lost the county but carried the territory. "That ought to settle Sanders," Will concluded. "It is the fourth time he came out behind. His office of attorney for the N.P.R.R. killed him. Working men are not apt to look for the principles, of either political party when . . . [they] see the agent of a gigantic monopoly running for office. With a good man the Reps. could have carried the territory." Actually, Sanders would make it to Washington as a result of the bizarre politics of the first state legislature, which was split evenly between the two parties. The rival assemblies each elected their own senators, but it was Republicans Sanders and Thomas C. Power who were finally seated by the U.S. Senate.

By year's end, Will had gotten his promotion to stationary

engineer. Not only was the pay a dollar better but he could get in more hours. He figured that his monthly wages would increase between 40 and 50 dollars. That extra money would make possible a trip he had been planning back East. Meanwhile, the unforgettable winter of 1886-87 was laying siege to the West, exacting a high toll in general misery and in livestock lost. In November, Will observed in his diary, "Cold weather struck us in earnest day before yesterday," and then later, "Snow commenced falling Xmas or the day before and did not stop for 3 or 4 days. More snow here now than I ever saw here before . . . . very cold the past week." Temperatures of 60 below were not unknown. Blizzards plugged the mountain passes and swept the high plains, piling cattle against the fences, decimating the herds. The great white death of 1886-87 ended the old cattle kingdom.

Spring brought preparations for Will's first trip back East since the family had uprooted from their Pennsylvania home. Finally leaving in June, he had several weeks of visiting relatives and friends around Scranton and New York." Met a large number of old-time friends," he recalled, "and also made many new ones." He was back in Butte by early September, in time to see Cousin Tommy again on his way through to Portland, Oregon.

Butte in 1887, or Montana Territory for that matter, had little to offer a young man with a passion for learning. The University System, with a unit in town, was still several years in the future. The little Presbyterian school over at Deer Lodge was struggling to help young people of the intermountain region, but Will had not yet found the reason to leave home. So, in the evening and at other available times, while many of his generation pursued the town's varied diversions, he read Schiller and Shakespeare, tried to fathom the mysteries of mathematics, studied rhetoric, and undertook to learn foreign languages. Always uncertain of himself because he lacked formal training, he would over the years acquire knowledge in a number of areas that was unrivaled by many university graduates.

Meanwhile, his ambition was beginning to focus on the law as a career. Among his friends was George M. Bourquin, later to sit on the federal bench where he acquired a reputation as a "tough judge" who could deal with court backlogs expeditiously. They became acquainted in the National Guard, in which Will served from 1888 to 1893. They also worked together in the mines, running engines and together they began to read law. Jameson became impatient with his progress and decided that if he became a

Rebecca Richards

stenographer for a lawyer he could get ahead more quickly. That meant going to school, to build upon the skills he had acquired during his ten-week shorthand course. He talked matters over with his mother, who was strongly supportive of her son's studious ways and his ambition for a career. She had enough boarders now to take care of the family, and the three girls were there to help with the cooking and house-work.

So Will enrolled in the Central Business College in Sedalia, Missouri for the fall term of 1889. That proved to be an eventful time in which to be away. His first letter from home told of a disastrous fire, fanned by high winds, that had ravaged part of Butte's business district on September 29th. But happier tidings came early in November when Montana at long last became the 41st state of the Union. Will hated not to be on hand for the big celebration on the 8th. But from Sedalia he echoed the sentiments sounded by the *Helena Daily Herald*: "Hurrah for Statehood! Hurrah! The State of Montana! That sounds good!" [8]

The special election in October, however, that ratified the constitution had also produced a crisis for the new state government. The governor was a Democrat but the Lieutenant-Governor was a Republican and could cast the tie-breaking vote in a senate evenly divided between the parties. The lower house also had an equal number of Democrats and Republicans, but the problem lay with the contested delegations from Silver Bow County. Both parties claimed the five legislative seats involved, and, when partisan differences could not be resolved, the lower house split into two assemblies. No laws were passed, while two sets of U.S. senators were elected, with the Republican choices finally being seated by the U.S. Senate. Montana was not alone in having to cope with such problems, but it did make for a shaky beginning.

State politics, Will reflected from Missouri, did run an uncertain course. The year before, in his bid to become territorial delegate, William Andrews Clark had felt confident of victory. After all, he was the Democratic nominee and his opponent a relative unknown. But fellow Democrat, Marcus Daly and his partners, evidently for business reasons, preferred a Republican in Washington. They conspired to shift votes to Thomas H. Carter, with such success that Silver Bow County, bastion of Democracy, went for Clark's Republican foe and helped send him to Washington. That fired the Clark-Daly feud, which embroiled Montana politics for years to come. Years later, in 1900, as Daly lay dying in the Netherlands Hotel in New York, his arch rival was still fuming over what he regarded as the great treachery of 1888.

In May of 1890, upon completion of his studies, Will received a letter of commendation which said in part: "He is the most accurate student in shorthand, considering the experience he has had, that we have ever known. He reads his notes almost as accurately as print. Added to this knowledge he has a fund of general information that but few young men of his age possess, and which will be of material benefit to him in his shorthand work. Mr. Jameson is a model in his moral character and sterling integrity.... Many things in his praise are left unsaid to avoid the appearance of exaggerating." [9]

Back in Butte, Will secured employment as a stenographer for

PROGRAM

9:00 Introductory Comments
Professor Cynthia Ford

9:15 The Federal Bench

9:15 - 10:00 - The federal selection process
Eleanor Acheson

10:00 - 10:30 - The 1996 Montana appointment
Judge Diane Barz, committee member
Bob James, committee member
Helena Maclay, appointment candidate

10:30 Break

10:40 The State Bench

10:40 - 11:20 - Getting Elected
Judge Diane Barz
Judge Kitty Curtis
Judge Marge Johnson
Judge Dorothy McCarter

11:20 - 12:00 - Getting Appointed
Judge Diane Barz, Judicial Nomination Commission
Bob James, Judicial Nomination Commission
Justice Karla Gray, judicial candidate
Karen Townsend, judicial candidate

Law Weekend '96

Symposium

Women and the Judicial Selection Process

The History of Women on the Bench in Montana

Saturday, April 20, 1996

9:00 - 12:00 a.m.

University of Montana School of Law

Sponsored By:

University of Montana Women's Law Caucus

&

Women's Law Section of the State Bar

Keynote Speaker:
Eleanor D. "Eldie" Acheson
Assistant Attorney General, U.S. Department of Justice

Ms. Acheson is responsible for the Clinton Administration's judicial selection process, working with the White House and the Senate to ensure a high quality federal judiciary.

A special *Thank-you* to the following supporters of The University of Montana Women's Law Caucus

Bitterroot Motors - Kathy Ogren
First Bank
KMSO "The Point" Sheila Callahan
Topp Travel - Phyllis Topp
MTB Management - Margaret Langel

Dedication Ceremony

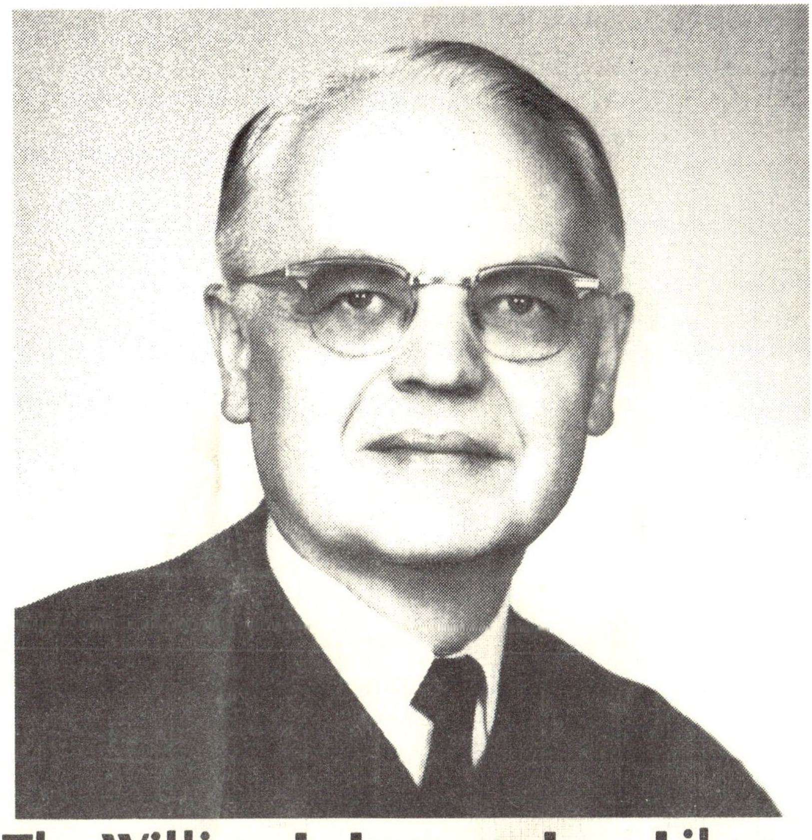

The William J. Jameson Law Library

The University of Montana

April 20, 1996

William J. Jameson

Judge William J. Jameson was born in Butte in 1898 and was raised in Roundup. After earning undergraduate and law degrees from The University of Montana, in 1922 he began—at $125 a month—35 years of legal practice in Billings with what is today the law firm of Crowley, Haughey, Hanson, Toole and Dietrich. In 1923 he married Mildred Lore.

While in private practice, Jameson served in the Legislature and on the Billings Board of School Trustees, chaired the Yellowstone County Chapter of the American Red Cross, and was a member of the boards of the Billings YMCA, Billings Deaconess Hospital, The University of Montana Foundation, and Rocky Mountain College. He also served as president of the UM Alumni Association and on the Board of Visitors for the School of Law. Jameson was associated with the law school for over 70 years, lecturing, judging competitions, and hiring its graduates as clerks.

In 1957, President Dwight D. Eisenhower appointed Jameson to be U.S. District Judge for Montana. He achieved senior status in 1969, and sat on appeals courts nationwide. In 1976 he was appointed by Chief Justice Burger to the Temporary Emergency Court of Appeals.

Jameson received the ABA Medal, the ABA's highest honor, in 1973. He had served as president of the ABA, and was a member of the American Judicature Society, the American Bar Endowment, the American Law Institute, the State Bar of Montana, and many other professional organizations. He chaired the ABA Section of Judicial Administration's Committee on Standards for Administration of Criminal Justice and was a member of the Conference of Commissioners on Uniform State Laws. After 30 years on the bench, Judge Jameson retired in 1987. He died October 8, 1990 at the age of 92. His contributions to his community, Montana, the Bar, and this law school were many.

Program

Processional

Welcome

Dean E. Edwin Eck
President George M. Dennison

Dedication Address

The Honorable James R. Browning

Video Presentation

The Life of Judge William J. Jameson

Musical Interlude

Katherine Honaker and
Ralph Sappington

Family Response

Mary J. Honaker
William J. Jameson, Jr.

Conclusion

Dean E. Edwin Eck

Recessional

Reception follows

Incidental Music Provided
by the Avalon String Trio

Law Clerks
to Judge William J. Jameson

Louis R. Moore
John V. Potter, Jr.
George C. Dalthorp
Edward W. Borer
Douglas C. Allen
Robert G. Anderson
Jeffrey J. Scott
Sam E. Haddon
Richard L. Beatty
J. Dwaine Roybal
Brent R. Cromley
Ronald F. Waterman
Rex B. Stratton, III
Harold V. Dye
Richard E. McCann
John F. Sullivan
J. Martin Burke
Joel Guthals
Allan Karell
William Rossbach
Christian D. Tweeten
James C. Kilbourne
Laura A. Mitchell
Erik B. Thueson
Tim D. Hall
Daniel N. McLean
Michael F. Lamb
C. Ken Sande
Shelley A. Hopkins
Peter F. Habein
Mickale C. Carter
Elaine Hightower Gagliardi
Ronald A. Nelson

Gifts to the Judge William J. Jameson Endowment for the use of the William J. Jameson Law Library may be made through The University of Montana Foundation, Missoula, MT 59812.

Carroll & Leahy, working there from 1890 to 1892 while he studied law. In the latter year, in addition to his regular job, he and two partners opened the Silver Bow News Company, handling such items as stationary, books, periodicals, and confections. The venture filled his evening hours but proved to be financially unwise. After six months, the partners were able to meet all obligations and close the store. Another of Will's interests at this time was the Sons of Veterans. He was instrumental in establishing the J.A. Garfield Camp, served as post captain in 1888-89, and then made his way through the ranks to be elected Commander of the Montana Division in 1892.

Following another trip back East, he took a stenographic position with Charles R. Leonard, while completing his legal studies. This proved to be a particularly interesting job, for Leonard would become a local attorney for F. Augustus Heinze, who, along with Clark and Daly, reigned as Butte's "copper kings." There Will had a close look at the secret maneuverings and legal shenanigans that were a part of Heinze's bold defiance of the mighty Amalgamated Copper Company. At length he was ready to take his bar examinations. The *Helena Herald* for June 29, 1896 reported that he was one of three to be successful and that he (along with Charles F. Word of Helena) "came in for especial creditable remarks," that their examinations were "especially meritorious." He was admitted to the State Supreme Court and, later, to the U.S. District Court and the Court of Appeals of the 9th circuit.

Will had not been too busy with his career preparations to keep an active interest in family happenings. He was there for sister Mary's graduation from Butte High School in 1895. It took real commitment to survive the occasion. Each member of the class had a speech to deliver during the day-long ceremonies. The program began at 9:30 A.M. and included six musical selections and fifteen speeches before lunch. At 2 P.M. came six more selections, fourteen speeches and, finally, the presentation of diplomas. High school education was of recent origin in Montana and a valued opportunity; apparently, no one was of a mind to hurry through this glad day of fruition.

III.

Two years earlier Butte High had graduated in a class of eleven one Annie J. Roberts, who stayed on for a post graduate normal training course and then became a teacher in town. It was a happy circumstance for the young lawyer who found in her the woman to stir his romantic nature. They would be married on August 14, 1897. Annie's roots were English. Her mother was born in Cornwall, one of ten children, and christened Charity Eva. A wealthy relative had promised to endow a namesake, but nothing came of it and little Charity was left with a name she would always detest.

Cornwall, jutting out into the Atlantic, was a land apart, a peninsula of rocky cliffs and wild uplands good for raising sheep and cattle. Its well-watered river valleys supported vegetable and dairy farming. Cornish tin and copper mines had been worked from ancient times. It was a region rich in legend, including that of King Arthur, and its rocky shores had long invited smuggling and piracy. Charity's family lived in Camborne on the western coast and, as a child, she remembered seeing smugglers unloading their boats and hiding the loot in caves. The ocean that laved the shores had always drawn young Cornishmen to sea as sailors, and also carried restless miners to the new world. There they were reluctant to let loose of their dialect, a blend of Welsh and Breton tongues, and it would be heard in Montana's mining camps. Charity, however, received her schooling in "paid" institutions where all were encouraged to use the proper "King's English." It was in Cornwall, in the mines near Camborne, that John Wesley sought converts to Methodism, preaching to people in the fields, and that persuasion became a part of the religious heritage of the Roberts and Jameson families.

Annie's father, Philip Roberts, came from bordering Devonshire, famous for forbidding Dartmoor, as well as for its "clotted" cream and the heavy accents of its people. Orphaned early in life, he faced a future of drudgery in the tin mines. Somehow books became his sole pleasure and the only means of gratifying a yearning for knowledge. Born in 1851, by the time he was twenty-one he had saved enough money to make the long trip to America and to the frontier territory of Montana. Here he joined other miners from Cornwall whose lusty and untutored voices, on a Saturday night, would roll through the gulches of the gold camps with strains of song from the world's great arias.

Philip returned home for a visit in 1874, when he met, courted, and persuaded Charity to come to the new world and be his bride. She was to leave the following year, to give him time to ready a Montana home. And though he had traveled steerage, she was to come first class. That proved to be rather embarrassing for the shy

Philip and Charity Eva

20-year old, trying to make do with her limited wardrobe as she mingled with the well-dressed passengers. She entrained from New York to Corrine, Utah and then took the stage coach north to Helena. That particular trip was regarded as one of the most tiresome by many western travelers, redeemed only by the sight of Montana's mountains or, for the treasure-seekers, the prospect of sudden riches.

For part of the way boredom was not a problem as Indians in warpaint trailed the coach, while the male passengers kept their guns in readiness. One of them was the Episcopal missionary bishop for the region, Daniel Tuttle, and he was rather intrigued by this young English woman of impeccable speech and beautiful black hair. Time and again he inquired why she was going to Montana, but Charity sweetly kept him guessing. Later, after the wedding, she met him again at a reception and was introduced as Mrs. Philip Roberts. "Ah," the bishop smiled, "just as I suspected," and thereafter he always referred to her as "the little English bride."

Their marriage at Helena on August 14th was reported in the *Helena Weekly Herald* for the 19th, along with a detailed description of the hanging of one William Wright Wheatley for the murder of Franz Warl. The execution was witnessed, the paper declared, by more than a thousand people and "is an event that will be long remembered, for the reason that he was the first and only man ever convicted of murder and hung in Montana by legal procedures."

In Unionville, not far from Helena, where Philip had settled, the newlyweds ate their first meal at the boardinghouse and then went to their two-room cabin. It was a cozy place in a yard with little evergreen trees, with space for a vegetable garden, and a brook separating them from the neighbors. A thoughtful friend gave them a feather mattress and also cooked their first meal while Charity unpacked their few possessions. That night the miners gathered for a charivari. Charity was prepared with plenty of food on hand. Attired in her favorite brown silk dress, she greeted them with "gentlemen" and was cheered by one and all.

Unionville was still a busy place with enough community spirit to raise $1000 for a Baptist church. There was also an Episcopal mission in town which Philip and Charity attended and sang in the choir. The "little English bride" took frontier life in stride, including the axing of a rattle-snake that had foolishly ventured upon her front porch. In time the mines would play out, cabins would be abandoned on the wooded hillsides, more and more buildings would be boarded up and Unionville would become another Montana ghost town. Meanwhile, Annie Jane joined the Roberts family on June 4, 1876, in the year of the nation's first centennial and three weeks before the fateful event on the Little Big Horn.

Philip did fairly well with his gold mining. One strike was particularly promising but, unfortunately, he had only an oral agreement on the mine and his lease was canceled. However, word spread as his discovery became one of the "lost leads" of the Union Whitlock mine. He mined enough gold to keep the family going and to cover medical expenses when he came down with "inflammatory rheumatism."

One of the most memorable times in Unionville came in the summer of 1877 when residents panicked at the rumors that Chief Joseph and the Nez Perce were heading that way on their escape to refuge in Canada. Already the Indians and Colonel Gibbons's troops had had a bloody encounter in the Big Hole Basin. Women and children were hidden in a mine tunnel. Philip gave Charity a revolver with instructions to use it on Annie and herself if the Indians broke in. Then it was learned that the fleeing Nez Perce had gone another way.

Annie was 18 months old when Philip decided to join brother Billy in his gold mine at Hassel. Billy had been so impressed with Charity that he asked her if there were any more like her back in Cornwall. She recommended sister Mary, whereupon he left for England, courted and married Mary and brought her back to Hassel. So it was a happy reunion for the sisters. The families prospered with the gold mine and times were generally pleasant. Little Annie would remember the Christmases at Hassel, with Charity making taffy in the shape of fishes. One Christmas in particular was unforgettable, when she left the new wax doll Santa Claus had brought too near the stove. The toy melted and Charity scolded her, pointing out that it had cost her father a lot of money. "Oh," Annie exclaimed, eyes brightening, "then you and Papa are Santa Claus!" And somehow that bit of revelation helped to ease the burden of her loss.

Billy was definitely one of the more colorful of the Roberts clan, quite unlike Philip who was gentle and soft-spoken. One morning, much the worse for a persistent toothache, he lost control of an unpredictable temper, grabbed hammer, chisel, and pliers and, in order to get even with the offending molar, extracted every tooth in his head! Mary heard the commotion and, coming into the kitchen, found her toothless spouse all spattered with blood. She was naturally timid and much too new to the frontier for such improvised measures and proceeded to faint. Billy carried her back to bed, where she had the good sense to stay until he had cleaned up the mess he had made.

On another occasion, Billy's terrible temper nearly cost him his scalp. He and a friend were out prospecting and stopped to have some flapjacks. A band of Indians happened by and invited themselves to the repast. Unfortunately, there seemed to be no filling them up and Billy tired of his occupation. A hapless Indian came back for one helping too many and Billy clobbered him with the pan of hot grease. Both prospectors were bound and taken to the chief who, luckily, thought the incident to be very funny and they were released.

In April of 1882 Roberts moved his family to a little house in Butte City. Annie was nearing school age and, besides, Charity had nearly died giving birth to their third child. A doctor was not available and the midwife had her limitations. Billy was sad and Mary tearful at the departure. But Mary prepared a big dinner for their last day in Hassel, while Charity sang her youngest to sleep. "That's not an English ballad you're singing, sister," Mary observed. "It shows you've been living in Confederate Gulch." Many years later, Charity would add her voice to southern melodies heard on the radio, including some tunes that took her back to Hassel days. With possessions piled high and the children perched on feather mattresses, they wagoned over to Butte City, spending one night along the way in Radersburg.

The little house on West Boardman Street Roberts had bought for his family had no trees, lawn, or flowers for Charity's loving care. She remembered the beautiful gardens her father had kept back home and resolved to do the best with what the yard in Butte had to offer. There were also open mine shafts in the vicinity, to be scrupulously avoided by the children, which sometimes trapped airborne hats on a windy day. Philip and Charity had agreed to attend the nearest church, and it proved to be the Mountain View Methodist Church just down the hill from their home. She had not been uncomfortable with her husband's Episcopalianism, but it was good to have the family raised in the faith Wesley had brought to her native Cornwall. Mountain View had an active Sunday school program. Another point of interest about the little church was the local gossip that its foundation stones had "gold values."

Roberts first worked in the silver mines and then tried some mining on his own, particularly at the Olive Branch south of town, before returning to one of the large companies. He also served as a deputy sheriff for a while. A red-letter day came on October 24, 1884 when he renounced allegiance to Victoria, Queen of Great Britain and Ireland and Empress of India. He valued his American citizenship, read widely (as did Charity) to keep informed, and followed the preference of his Cornish countrymen in joining the Republican Party.

Tensions were strong between the Irish and the Cornishmen, making for friction in the mines and numerous barroom brawls. Somehow Roberts managed to live in peace with his Irish neighbors, Republican and Mason though he was, while they embraced the Democracy and belonged to the Knights of Columbus. Eventually, animosities lessened between these two strong rival elements in Butte and they would even intermarry and share in each other's favorite occasions of St. Patrick's and St. George's days.

Charity presided over a busy household and set a table which her children and grandchildren would long remember. Her Cornish "pasties" (beef pies) were a favorite item for the family and for Philip's lunch bucket. No one bettered her potato salad, served with cold ham or cold roast beef. She also had a way with "Irish potatoes," doctored with butter and cream. The cookie jar was always full, and there were the saffron cakes and chocolate cake with icing almost as thick as the layers and topped with walnuts. One and all were encouraged to eat heartily and speak well of the place.

The holidays were a special time for the English immigrants in Butte. They kept open house, with each family having a big party, featuring roast pork, fruit cakes, fancy cakes, nuts and candy. With the coming of the railroads, fruit was more available and was added to the menu. Charity welcomed the holidays as an opportunity to set two tables to accommodate the family and friends. And when all had feasted to their satisfaction and the dishes were done, there was the singing, so dear to their hearts, of the old-time favorites along with the popular current tunes."Put on Your Old Gray Bonnet" was sure to set feet to tapping around the room.

For Annie Butte City offered an exciting change from the little mining camp at Hassel. Early adventures included wandering into Chinatown and becoming thoroughly frightened because the Chinese talked in sing-song voices and laughed when they saw that she was lost. Or, there was the time when she had been left alone to care for the children and some of the "landless" Indians from the ghetto south of town came by demanding food. They wanted bisquits, but Annie was able to satisfy them with a box of crackers. On one occasion, when Charity was home, an intoxicated visitor eyed her black hair in a way that made for considerable uneasiness, until he accepted some bisquits and went on his way. Since Annie's father had to work and her mother was busy at home, she often had the assignment of doing the shopping. That provided other adventures from time to time and, also, an acquaintance with a friendly butcher who called her "Miss Roberts" and gave her a slice of bologna with each purchase.

School brought more friends, including Molly Daly, daughter of the rising copper king. Often when the coachman came by school

Annie Roberts upon Graduation from Butte High School, 1893

to get Molly, he would give Annie a ride and so she would arrive home in style. At other times, when she walked, she liked to wander through vacant lots in search of wild flowers for a little bouquet for her mother. Sunday school at Mountain View was an important part of her life, and especially memorable were the annual picnics. The church chartered a train to take the children to a picnic spot beyond Homestake and it was an all day affair.

During her high school years, Annie endeavored to earn some pocket money. One summer she kept a kindergarten but her charges were so low that she made only fifteen dollars. Somewhat more profitable was her job as an errand girl in a millinery shop. One day a carriage load of women with lots of powder and paint on their pretty faces came by to purchase expensive hats. They noticed the young girl with the admiring eyes and gave her a huge bottle of cologne. Annie was impressed but not the shop owner, who thereafter saw that she had errands to do whenever the "ladies of the night" came around.

She graduated with high grades on May 12, 1893. The *Daily Intermountain* described the occasion for its readers. "When the curtain was raised a lovely picture was shown. The class motto 'Honor Waits at Labor's Gates' adorned the entrance in the rear, which was draped in lace. The eleven young high school graduates sat in a semi-circle. . . . The young ladies were all tastily attired in white. . . . Miss Annie J. Roberts spoke on 'English Literature in the High School.' The young woman has a splendid clear delivery and the entertaining manner in which she discussed the subject indicated exhaustive study and research. Miss Roberts' paper was exceedingly good and was well received by an intelligent and appreciative audience." Annie's white silk dress had taken most of the available cash, but Philip and Charity found enough more to send her a lovely bouquet. The *Daily Intermountain* noted that after the exercises some of the alumni took the graduates to Mrs. Neidemhofen's cafe for refreshments and a light luncheon.[10]

The headlines that summer, in Butte and elsewhere, would belong to the deepening economic crisis in the land, the Panic of 1893. Since 1890 the government's gold reserves had been declining, due in part to restrictive tariffs and to private hoarding of the precious metal. But for President Cleveland and eastern moneyed interests, the problem lay with the monetization of silver. So he called the Congress into special session in the fall of 1893 and won repeal of the Sherman Silver Purchase Act, halting government buying of silver. Fear bred fear as silver mines in Butte and elsewhere locked their gates, businesses folded, and the ranks of the unemployed grew to alarming proportions in the land. In Montana, one-third of the work force was idled by year's end.

The hard times lasted and split the nation between the western silverites and the eastern "goldbugs," pointing the country toward the great silver crusade and re-aligning election of 1896. Meanwhile, many of Montana's silver mines closed for good, leaving a few forlorn buildings victim to the elements and the annual visits of thoughtless tourists intent upon accumulating fragments from the past.

IV.

Following her post-graduate normal training course, Annie taught in the Butte schools from 1894 to 1897. She combined with her duties a rather active social life. Her outgoing personality was revealed in eyes that usually sparkled and in a warm, pleasant face. She had many friends and on one occasion she and sister Eva decided to visit some acquaintances who lived a ways out of town. That meant hiring a carriage. Unfortunately, the horse had been conditioned to stopping at saloons and he didn't miss one along the route! The only way the young women could get him going again was to step out of the carriage and then in again, much to their annoyance and to the amusement of the saloon clientele.

Much more pleasurable was her meeting a young lawyer named William J. Jameson. He began taking her to dances and to the theater and soon it appeared that their courtship was in earnest. Annie's people liked Will and the idea of having a barrister in the family. Philip teased his daughter by observing that young Jameson had good sense enough to go home when he began winding the clock!

Will was now 32, eleven years older than Annie, serious and settled in his ways, kindly and gentle but yet ready to protect the young woman he was courting with the derringer he carried in his pocket! They were married on August 14, 1897 at the Roberts home on West Boardman Street, with the Methodist minister officiating. Jameson almost did not make it on time, in his concern to finish the work at the office that morning. But, a little out of breath, he was there in his cutaway to stand beside his bride, radiant in her white silk dress with orange blossoms in her hair. For the honeymoon he had planned an extended trip back East, one which challenged all of Annie's ingenuity in getting her dresses and all those petticoats jammed into a small steamer trunk. Her travels to date had been limited to trips between the mining camps and a few weeks on a ranch near Fish Creek. So the wedding journey was a thing of great anticipation.

Annie Roberts Jameson, 1897

Amidst plenty of sightseeing, including Niagara Falls, the Jamesons worked in visits to the National Camp of the Patriotic Order of the Sons of America and the affiliated order of the Daughters of America at Reading, Pennsylvania and the G.A.R. Encampment at Buffalo, New York. There was all the numerous Jameson clan to be visited in both states, with the New York relatives going out of their way in showing the newly weds the sights of the big city. The Metropolitan Museum of Art made a particularly vivid impression. On the way home, they stopped at Chicago to see the Libby Prison War Museum which had been located there several years earlier. Will was silent as he pondered the tragedy of the father he had never known but whose name he bore.

Back in Butte after a month's travels, they purchased a little house on West Quartz Street and shopped around for furnishings. A sewing machine for Annie cost $24.50 and a kitchen range $37.50. A dresser and chair added another $15 and a rocker $5.50. It said something about the young couple's values that their most expensive investment was a Camp & Co. piano at $240. Jameson returned to his work at Charles R. Leonard's office and Annie began a new career as homemaker. On August 8 of 1898 a son was born and named William James, Jr. and then two years later a daughter Lucille. The lines had met from Northern Ireland and from Cornwall in a new generation of Jamesons, endowed with a bit of frontier heritage and firmly rooted in Montana soil.

CHAPTER TWO

CHILDHOOD

Butte in the year of William Jameson's birth was known as "the metropolis of Montana," outdistancing all other cities in population and wealth. In fact, Butte claimed to be the largest city in the five-state region of Montana, Wyoming, Idaho, and the Dakotas. Once it had been said that the mining camp was good for a few years only, but that was before the discovery of immense mineral resources and the coming of copper as king. The census for 1900 found 30,470 in the city and 47,635 in Silver Bow County (about 20 percent of the states's population). By 1910 Butte had climbed to nearly 40,000 and the county to over 56,000.[1] Silver Bow's assessed valution stood at 27 million in 1897, compared to under 5 million in 1881. Residents surveyed such growth with notable satisfaction (and no little condescension towards lesser Montana towns), and, in general, regarded Butte as among the leading cities of the West.

Providence was conspiring, in the *Butte Miner's* view, to help Montana forget the recent hard times. Ranchers and woolgrowers were benefitting from improved market conditions, while the mines were helping to generate a monthly payroll of one million for the city. There were, by that newspaper's report, 10,000 workers in the mines as the new year of 1898 came around, up 2100 over the previous year![2] Rivalry between the copper kings was redounding to labor's benefit, with Clark, and then Heinze, giving their miners an eight-hour day, at a time when that concession was enjoyed by only 8 percent of the industrial workers in the country. Unionism in Butte fared well, while industrial strife was making the headlines elsewhere in the land. Soon that situation would change, for the purchase of the Anaconda by Standard Oil in 1899 would mean big trouble for unionism later on.

Meanwhile, Butte was fairly euphoric with its prospects. "Butte busy if not beautiful," the *Miner* declared, suggesting that though the pristine loveliness George Porter had found in the early days was gone that was the necessary price of progress. Presiding at the Constitutional Convention in 1889, William A. Clark had observed, in a rare moment of humor, that Butte women did not need cosmetics, for there was enough arsenic in the air to give them beautiful complexions.

But Butte was more than "the greatest mining camp on earth." In the *Miner's* inventory at the beginning of 1898, she was "a city of prosperity, progress, and happiness," her citizens enjoying "all the modern improvements which go to make up a city of metropolitan pretensions." Public buildings and many private residences were being constructed of brick and stone to "bid defiance to time." Even so, the *Miner* affirmed, they would crumble in dust before the mines of the "richest hill on the earth" would be exhausted. Butte could be proud of her splendid hotels, perhaps the finest library (the *Miner* averred) in the West, a public power plant nearing completion at a cost of $300,000, and streets and railroads reaching all the suburban towns. Prosperity seemed to be assured. "What was true of 1897," the *Miner* reasoned, " should be doubly true of 1898."[3]

So the times seemed to be much improved as Will and Annie waited for their first-born. The public schools were enrolling 5,000 children, with another 1,000 attending private institutions. To be sure, most would not make it beyond the eighth grade, and that fact stirred some criticism when a new high school was built for $125,000. With the average miner on the hill earning more than the teachers, there was little incentive, aside from personal ambition, for most boys to pursue an education. For the industrious ones, however, Butte had grabbed a piece of the university system when it was organized in 1893. A wary legislature minimized the political fallout by opting for a multi-unit system. In addition to the School of Mines at Butte, there was the University at Missoula, the Agricultural College at Bozeman, and the Normal College at Dillon.

Along with all that was positive and praiseworthy as the new year came around, the *Miner* and other papers voiced continuing concern over the city's coarse side. Both gambling and prostitution were, in effect, being licensed through a system which allowed the posting and forfeiture of bonds. On the theory that these social evils could not be eradicated, the police chief collected the fines and pocketed his ten percent commission. From the Garden City, the *Missoulian* issued a barbed reminder that gambling was a felony under state law, which applied even to Butte despite that city's pretension of being "greater than Montana."[4] It was time for the city fathers to end the licensing of vice there. A "triple alliance" of county attorney, sheriff, and police did mount a concerted effort in raiding the gambling houses, but they met with little success in trying to curb the interminable fall of the cards or the pursuit of pleasure in the "badlands" of Galena Street.

The Butte Ministerial Association joined in the crusade against vice, though the clergy cast a wider net to include Sunday places of amusement. Theaters should be closed on Sunday evenings and band concerts forbidden on the day of rest. The latter, however, touched a particularly sensitive nerve, for the city was proud of its bands. Sam Treloar from Leadville, Colorado had organized the Boston & Montana band in 1887 and built it into an organization which won national acclaim. Butte was not about to restrict its enjoyment of concerts and parades.

II.

By early August the papers were filled with news of the ending of the Spanish-American War. Yellow journalism had stirred jingoistic spirits in Butte, as elsewhere, and then came Dewey's heady victory at Manila Bay, the dash for glory up San Juan Hill, and the blasting of Spain's decrepit fleet off Cuba. But if few Americans fell in battle, thousands in their woolen uniforms succumbed to tropical heat, bad food, and disease. Families everywhere were glad to hear that Spain was ready to call it quits. On August 8th, as Madrid weighed Washington's terms for surrender, Annie Jameson gave birth to a son. The next day's newspaper reported: "Born—August 8, to wife of W.J. Jameson, at 930 West Quartz Street, a 9½ pound boy."

Two years later, on August 21, daughter Lucille joined a closely-knit family that included two sets of grandparents, two uncles, and six aunts. In that extended circle of relationship, the new Jamesons would seldom lack for attention or affection. Each noon, with quick stride, the young attorney covered the 14 blocks from his office to his home, ate a hurried lunch, hummed his children to sleep with a tuneless "um-um," and then returned to C.R. Leonard — all in one hour! Will was not much for athletics, but he kept his body of medium height and weight in good shape with frequent walking.[5]

The happy, loving young housewife often sang as she prepared the meals and cleaned the little place on West Quartz Street. Lucille was nearly grown before she discovered that "Three Little Maids from School Are We" was from the *Mikado* and not an original composition by her mother for her daughter and two close friends. Annie was often at her piano and later would play at church, after the move to Roundup. Will and Annie on occasion exposed their children to the cultural life of the city. Willie, as he was called, and Lucille were 5 and 3 when they were first introduced to *Faust*.

Three days a week Annie ordered groceries from the "solicitor" who came around. At other times Chinese venders came by with buckets of produce attached to poles carried on their shoulders. They were welcomed by the children, since they handed out candy treats on such special occasions as the Chinese New Year. But, perhaps, most enjoyable for young and old alike were the summertime outings at Columbia Gardens, three and a half miles east of town in the foothills of the Continental Divide. In 1899, in a moment of rare generosity for the area where he had made his fortune, William A. Clark built a trolley park on 80 acres of beautifully landscaped ground. Formal flower beds provided a profusion of colors, while an acre of pansies was an invitation for children to pick a bouquet for mother.

On Thursdays it was "Children's Day" at the Gardens, complete with free transportation from town. On one occasion, in May of 1907, 10,000 children and their parents were trained in from around the region to see Butte's famous amphitheater, compliments of Mr. Clark. The Gardens included a pavilion where dance bands performed and an athletic field with grandstand for baseball and football as well as for "hammer and drill" drilling contests when the miners displayed their skills.[6] The Jamesons, with aunts, uncles, and grandparents, planned as many picnics as possible for the Gardens. Rebecca and Charity would spread out their table clothes and produce from their baskets such delectables as fried chicken, potato salad, and thickly-layered chocolate cake. Those full and happy days of summer often extended into the evening hours when the pavilion opened and the grown-ups could get in a few waltzes before it was time to get the young ones to bed. On the way home, however, there was often one more stop at the ice cream parlor for a final snack.

Especially memorable for Willie was the time when he was deemed old enough to ride the street cars alone, or even have Lucille entrusted to his care. On occasion, as he rode the cars from his west side home to the center of the town, he met colorful Judge William Clancy, reportedly copper king Heinze's man on the district bench. The bearded, tobacco-chewing judge took a liking to young Jameson and routinely handed him a nickel, which prompted Willie to schedule his rides to benefit from Clancy's generosity.

Summer also meant baseball for Willie and his pals, organized without benefit of sponsors or coaches and played in a vacant lot without patronizing parents on the sidelines. Neighborhood teams made up the "league," with Willie's West Side Sluggers having a particularly strong rivalry with the boys from Dublin Gulch. They were frequent adversaries and victory was especially savored and talked over at the dinner table. Winter also had its diversions, sledding on the nearby slopes, cheeks rosy and tingly with Butte's invigorating, mile-high cold, or skating with friends at the city rink.

As the only grandchildren, Willie and Lucille fared well at Christmas, including two dinners with the grandparents. It was something of a challenge for young stomachs, though, to go from Grandma Roberts' table at noontime to do justice to Grandma Richards' feast at suppertime. Rebecca had married once more. Joseph Richards was a foreman at the Leonard Mine and had been a boarder since 1885. He introduced the children to Pantages vaudeville and each Saturday morning gave them money for the afternoon matinee. Eventually, Willie and Lucille tired of the routine and convinced him to spend his money on something else. Grandpa Roberts taught them how to pan for gold. His gentle, kindly ways drew the children to him, and few holidays passed without a card or gift from him.

Willie's first foray into the world of business, at the tender age of five, earned him an uncharacteristic scolding from Grandma

Richards. Her sister, Hannah, had come for a visit and Rebecca was bragging how clean and well dressed Annie always kept the children. Unfortunately, that was the day when Willie and friend, Eddie Downey, decided to enter the trash collection trade. By the time they reached Grandma Richards' house they had already made a trip or two to the dump with their carts and their efforts were evident in badly smudged hands, faces, and clothes. Instead of getting Rebecca's business, of which they had been confident, Willie received a tongue-lashing he would long remember, terminating not only the garbage collection business but, perhaps, nipping any latent instincts for the world of trade!

Across the street lived the Jewish rabbi who ministered to the 500 or so Jews living in Butte at the turn of the century. They were part of the "new immigration," after 1880, flooding in from Southeastern Europe, including dark-skinned Slavs and Italians. Annie was friendly with the rabbi's wife, and little son, Abie, played with Willie and Lucille, though he was some years younger. Abie was often the butt of discrimination, which prompted Willie to assume the role of defender and to sometimes use his fists. To some extent, McKinley School reflected the "melting pot" that was Butte—the mix of nationalities, the poor and the orphaned along with the children of the more comfortably situated West Side families. Something in the early education of Willie Jameson would season into those qualities of kindness and concern for fair play that later marked his life and career.

Will Jameson kept to a busy schedule at C.R. Leonard's law firm, but on weekends he found relaxation in building houses. He sold the first one but then moved his family from the small dwelling on Quartz Street to a new four-bedroom house he had constructed two blocks away on West Copper Street. In the backyard he built a little replica of the new residence as a playhouse for Lucille, completed in time for her seventh birthday. There she could observe the happy occasion by serving ice cream and cake to a few envious friends!

The new home, of course, called for additional furnishings. That worried Annie when two detectives came by one day to inquire if Will had any knowledge of where a Heinze employee had secured money for an extravagant style of living, including frequent trips to the race track. After they had left, Annie voiced concern that they might be suspicious of the Jameson's new surroundings. However, Will was able to assure her that they were not living in such lavish manner as to invite investigation.

III.

The Butte years were a time of contentment for the young family, with the close relational ties and a growing circle of friends, but Will's work at C.R. Leonard was becoming more and more demanding. His salary was not commensurate with the growing responsibilities, especially during Mr. Leonard's lengthy absences from town. The firm was involved in the secret negotiations between Heinze and the Amalgamated. Among Will's papers was a telegram in code from the Heinze attorney in New York telling of the sale of the Butte properties to Amalgamated, before it was made public in February of 1906.

Will had also reached 40 and felt that it was time to open his own law office. Among the possible locations, two towns led to visits, to Whitefish and to Roundup, with the latter winning out. The Milwaukee Railroad had arrived in that coal town in 1907 and boom years appeared to lie ahead. The Jamesons spent the summer of 1908 there, living in a tent, while Will began to organize his practice. With the resiliency of youth, Willie and Lucille adapted quickly to the change and found tent-living quite the adventure. For Annie, however, the move from Butte would be a painful time, the wrenching of the uprooting from all that was familiar and pleasant and secure. The new home in Butte had all the conveniences of the day and, though tenting was a temporary expedient, she knew that living in Roundup would be different. Yet if that was what her husband wanted, she would be a willing part of this new beginning.

That fall Annie and the children returned to Butte for the school year, while Will made plans for their permanent relocation and got his law practice under way. The one-time roundup center of the Musselshell Valley was astir with activity. *The Roundup Record,* in its initial issue (April 3, 1908) observed that the town "is fast assuming a metropolitan appearance and ere long will have passed thru the stage which all new towns have to contend with, into the realm of citydom with substantial buildings, up-to-date improvements and other conveniences which tend to make life more pleasant."

Daily, the paper noted, the trains were bringing in "an army of home-seekers, laborers and businessmen." In addition to the coal mines, first opened in 1907, the country around Roundup provided much in the way of other natural resources. The bottom land of the Musselshell, *The Record* pointed out, offered soil as good as any for grains, alfalfa and sugar beets. The bench land further back from the river was ideal for homesteading and was rapidly being filed on. The cattle industry, which had first given the place its name, continued as an important part of the economy, and with the coming of the Milwaukee, bawling herds would be driven down Main Street to be loaded at the railroad siding on the east end of town. The Bull Mountains to the south were hardly the Continental Divide, but with their growth of pine they were keeping two saw mills busy supplying the needs of the mines and the town. If Billings 50 miles away over a rough and dusty road was calling itself the "Magic City," Roundup was soon claiming the title—the "Miracle of the Musselshell."

The population was mostly young and polyglot. Coal miners from southern Europe, the "hunks," worked beside the migratory ones from England, Scotland and Wales. Homesteaders came from all over but included soil-seekers from Scandinavia, Russia, and Germany. From the open range days, there were Scottish sheepgrowers and English ranchers. One of the most colorful ranchers became a client and a good friend. Lord Harold A. Lowther had come in the 1880's and established the NF Ranch near Roundup. His outgoing personality contrasted with his partner's, the Hon. Cecil Clifton (later Baron Grey de Ruthven) who stayed close to the ranch but could occasionally be coaxed away to give a piano concert. When Lord Lowther and the Baron went on an African safari one winter, they tried to get the Jamesons to stay at their luxuriously furnished ranch-house, offering the services of their Chinese cook, but Annie was not enthused about living out of town; besides, there was the problem of getting the children to school.

Many tongues were heard in the new town, along with the sounds of clashing customs, the feuds and barroom brawls, and not infrequent shootings. One of the most publicized murders occurred outside of town on March 27, 1908. Sheriff James T. Webb of Yellowstone County had ridden over from Billings to apprehend one William C. Bickford, an alleged horse thief from Wyoming. He found him in a sheepherder's wagon on the Woolfolk and Richardson ranch. Bickford grabbed a gun and mortally wounded the sheriff, but was hunted down by a posse and killed. A reporter from Butte sized up Roundup as "Rough, Ready, and Redolent," while the Associated Press later confided to the *Roundup Record* that more "juicy news" came from that town than from any other place in Montana, Butte included![7]

Home in Roundup

By June of 1909, the *Record* was reporting a population of 1500 and boasting that Roundup had achieved incorporation sooner than any other city in the state. Two main streets were graded and macadamized and soon would be lined with cement sidewalks. In the offing were a water works and an electric light plant that would be a credit to a much larger city. Of particular interest to the Jamesons was the completion of a four-room school house and the employment of three teachers to handle a projected enrollment of 160 children.

Will rented a comfortable three-bedroom house, the best that Roundup had to offer, but without plumbing. The nearest good well was several blocks away, and that meant pumping and hauling pails of water on a wagon or sled. The family collected rainwater for bathing and cleaning and adjusted to the inconveniences. Within a year Will bought their own home.

It meant a lot to them to have a new Methodist-Episcopal church. It was the first sanctuary in town, though the Episcopalians, Congregationalists, and Roman Catholics were also on the scene and planning for edifices within the year. The *Record* for June 25, 1909 reported the dedication of the new church on the previous Sunday. The day was rainy and the roads muddy, but the day-long observances were well attended. Rev. William W. Van Orsdel, superintendent of the Great Falls district, was the main speaker. Brother Van, as the beloved clergyman had been called since his arrival at Fort Benton back in 1872, gave both the morning and evening sermons. His latter address on "The Lost Vision" was delivered, the *Record* noted, "to the great delight of all."

Brother Van was a visitor in the Jameson home whenever he came to Roundup. Among other things, Annie had a way with chicken that was especially appealing. His appreciation of her culinary talents was no small matter as, over the years, he had sampled the fare of many Montana kitchens. Later, Willie would recall that Brother Van also took those occasions to urge him and Lucille to consider church vocations. The contagious good will of this unlettered man of God touched the hearts of most he met, the highly-placed and the bruised ones, his "diamonds in the rough." Perhaps Charlie Russell said it best in his letter to Brother Van on the occasion of his 70th birthday celebration at Fort Benton. "I have met you many times . . . Brother Van, sometimes in lonely places, but you never were lonesome or alone, for a man with scarred hands and feet stood beside you and near Him there is no hate, so all you met loved you." So it was that the Jamesons always looked forward to his visits.

All the family attended church, but Annie was especially involved, teaching in the Sunday school and often serving as organist. During the cold months, to save on the church's heating bill, the choir rehearsed at the Jameson home. The male section was mostly composed of Welsh miners from Klein, whose lusty voices could be heard of a winter's night as they drove up, sleighbells ringing, for choir practice.

In 1910 the fourth annual session of the North Montana Conference of the Methodist Episcopal Church met in Roundup. No one could figure what the minister had in mind in inviting the Conference to such a small church and town, but members were resolved to show the world that Roundup would not be found wanting. Congregationalists and Episcopalians made beds available to their Methodist neighbors and the housing emergency was handled. In the Jameson home, however, a minor crisis evolved. Annie thought that she and Will should move to an unfinished room upstairs so that the district superintendent and his wife could occupy their bedroom. Will flatly refused. He was busy at the office and there was a term of court at hand and he wanted his comfortable bed. The hotel proprietor owed him some money and he would put the superintendent there free of charge. Though Annie felt that it was hardly hospitable and wondered what the church members would think, Will held firm. As it happened, the arrangements were evidently quite satisfactory, for the superintendent wrote later expressing his appreciation for the fine accommodations.

Will and Annie had their disagreements, but nothing strained the devotion for each other that was deep and abiding. And that anchored the home life that meant so much to their children. Their affection was shown not so much in public caresses as in the things they did for each other. Will liked a piece of devil's food cake for breakfast, and Annie made sure that he was seldom without "Old Reliable," as he called it. On Sundays he did the breakfast dishes so that Annie could prepare for her class. He never forgot their anniversaries, even if finances dictated that he give her a single rose! When Annie was visiting in Butte, he would write daily, mostly in a humorous vein. Once when she was with Aunt Mary in Hassel and heard that Will had had a fall, she wrote: "I think you need me to take care of you . . . Your loving Annie." That was about as demonstrative as a young Victorian wife could be!

Annie's influence on her children was especially strong in their religious nurture. She taught Willie's Sunday school class through all the years to his graduation from high school in 1915. Her brand of Methodism was seasoned with a "social gospel" concern for the poor and needy and with the liberal leanings of such prominent churchmen as Bishop Francis J. McConnell and Dr. Harry F. Ward. She read from their writings to her class in the little Methodist church on the Musselshell. God's love was more real for Annie than his wrath. Once when a touring evangelist was at the church preaching hell-fire and damnation, she stood at the organ and interrupted with the firm declaration: "That is not what I teach my boys. I tell them of God's love!" Annie felt further vindication of her views when it was disclosed that the traveling exhorter had left a sizeable collection of empty whiskey bottles in his hotel room!

The Roundup years were full and satisfying for Willie and Lucille. Both skipped one grade in school and stayed at the top of their classes. Willie's was the second class, numbering 13, to graduate from the high school. He was senior class president and valedictorian. There was no athletic program in those first years, but he headed the school's literary society and was active in debate. What pleased the elder Jameson most was that his son won a district championship in debate that last year in school. In addition to his developing forensics skills, he was blessed with what one speaker from the university described as "a million dollar voice."

Willie's interest in debate had been sparked by the English teacher, Miss Josephine Sutherland, who also coached the team. She had come to the area, as had so many young teachers of the time, to file on a homestead but was making a major contribution in the classroom. Hers was an important influence upon young Jameson in sharpening his interest in literature as well as encouraging his forensics talents. Later, he would recall her with deep appreciation and remember her as one of the finest teachers he had had at any level of his learning!

Aside from school, the town offered a variety of diversions. For the culturally-minded, there was the annual visit of the Chautauqua Society. Entertainers and patrons filled a huge tent and suffered with the summer heat. Yet, the lectures, plays, and music groups were of such caliber as to make the experience worthwhile. Summer also meant the circus with a chance for Willie and his friends to obtain tickets by carrying water to the animals. The Ladies' Aids of the town took the opportunity to earn money selling food to the people flocking in from around the county. On one occasion, however, they were victimized by a short-change artist and ended with only a few dollars for all their efforts. Then too, there was the big Fourth of July celebration and parade and the popular rodeo events.

Before the coming of the automobile, there were always the livery stables in small towns like Roundup and the depot as places where people met to swap gossip or, perhaps, transact some business. Incoming trains merited the attention of a reporter, along with the idlers, to garner the latest news. But more than that, the Milwaukee tokened the town's prosperity and held its hopes for the future. It nurtured its commerce, as it also carried families "back east" for a visit or students to the university in Missoula. Young people walked its rails on a summer afternoon's adventure and speculated about the world beyond the Musselshell. Little wonder that in a distant day when those tracks were ripped away there would be a deep sadness in the hearts of the old-timers.

It wasn't far to the edge of town, to the dry coulees and sage brush, the yucca and the jackpines. There, perhaps at day's ending, in a moment of solitude, one might watch the sunset splashing colors on the rimrocks with consummate artistry. For the diligent searcher, a short hike might be rewarded with a patch of wild flowers, possibly a partially concealed treasure of white violets. That kind of discovery excited Lucille, while Willie and his pals were more apt to be hiking just to feel the freedom of the land. Or, they might be in quest of frogs. Frog legs were considered quite the delicacy, and he had acquired some proficiency in preparing them. His reputation, it seems, rested upon Annie's willingness to let him use generous amounts of butter in making the batter.

Willie also pursued his interest in baseball, with his neighborhood team frequently engaging the boys from Klein. Since there were few automobiles and no streetcars, that could mean a walk of four miles. Sunday was, perhaps, the most predictable day of the week, beginning with his mother's class, then church, and in the evening the Epworth League. That active young peoples' group had fund raising efforts from time to time, and Willie's contribution was making pineapple sherbet, with his mother as the main customer. However, when Annie served some to her company, her son's sherbet business grew.

One summer Willie had an opportunity to work in a local garage, handling the bookkeeping responsibilities, but his father discouraged him from taking it. The elder Jameson recalled his own hard struggle and was inclined to overcompensate in wanting life easier for his son. More than anything else, he wanted Willie to have that college education he had missed. In every way they could, he and Annie nurtured in their children a love of learning. They set the example in filling spare moments with reading. Family conversation ranged widely over literature, religion, history, politics and other topics.

Some time around 1913, Will decided to enter the automobile age. He was not impressed with Henry Ford's gift to civilization and went to Billings in search of a larger and heavier car. In the "Magic City" he encountered an old Butte neighbor who allowed that he had just what Will needed. It was a secondhand Marion, with low mileage and in excellent condition and he would give his friend a good price. It just so happened that the Butte man had business in Roundup and he offered to give Will a demonstration ride home. The Marion seemed to fit the bill and so the deal was made.

That trip from Billings, however, was the last one Will would make in his "new" car. Every subsequent effort ended in breakdowns or, on one or two occasion, near disaster. The auto mechanics in the area were just learning their trade and had frequent opportunity to practice on "Old Marion," whose mileage, it proved, had been badly misrepresented. Members of the Jameson family routinely took a book along to read, certain that "Old Marion" would fail them and that there would be time to kill while Will walked to the nearest ranch house to put in another garage call. The repair bills mounted and eventually, after the move to Missoula, Will parted with his "lemon," deciding that it was more important for the family to have money for food. "Old Marion" was later used in the rum-running business and, not unexpectedly, its unfortunate owner was caught!

For Willie, growing up in Butte and Roundup, there was never the choice posed by the poet of "two roads diverged in a yellow wood." For him, as really for Robert Frost, there was only one way to be taken. Since early childhood he had known that he wanted to follow in his father's footsteps and become a lawyer. In Roundup he waited for the visiting judge from Billings or Lewistown to hold court in town, and he was usually in attendance whether or not his father was involved in a case. He visited his father's law office, to the limits of the elder Jameson's patience, and was always attentive when his father had something to share from his practice during the suppertime conversations.

The fall of his junior year in high school he prepared an English III theme on the subject of "Law." He received an A+ for his efforts and Miss Sutherland's comment: "The best thing you have written." "Law is a profession," Willie began, "for which more study and perseverance is required than for any other walk of life. Not only this, but many virtues and good qualities are essential to a successful lawyer."

Written with clear penmanship, the paper proceeded to delineate the essentials for a successful legal practice. There was no substitute for a knowledge of the law, acquired, necessarily, by "years of hard labor and study." In addition, a good memory was "imperative," to be able to remember "all that is testified to by witnesses as well as all that is said by . . . [one's] opponent. Closely connected with memory is the power of perception. A lawyer who fails to note everything which takes place during a trial is at a great disadvantage." That perception must include how the judge and jury are responding, so that the attorney will not say anything prejudicial to his client, including saying too much." "The notion seems to prevail that a lawyer should be a fluent talker. But an attorney who employes all of the bombast he can . . . is not as successful as the one who talks forcibly, yet in simple language."

For Willie, courage was another quality of the successful lawyer. "The rulings of the court, the strength of his opponent and witnesses, the failings of his own witnesses, and other discouraging things, will continually disappoint the attorney. To be able to bear all of these things and many times face defeat requires steady nerve and a strong determination." But equally important was to be possessed of integrity. "In no profession is there such a temptation and such a chance to yield to trickery and deception. Yet to eventually succeed, an attorney must at all times be honest. He must first be honest with his client and advise him correctly as to his legal rights in the case. He must also be honest with the court, the jury, and with his adversary."

Willie's attorney also eschewed pride lest he not forget himself "in the interests of his client." In summary, he found that in "law, as in everything, you get out of it just what you put in. If a student has been diligent in his training and endeavored in every way to acquire those qualities essential to the law he will have a successful career and the prospects for such attorneys are bright. But for a poor lawyer there is not much chance as the field is somewhat crowded. It is a well known fact that there are many lawyers barely making a living. . . . But even now there is a demand for attorneys who know the law, respect it, and obey it."[8]

Clearly, his father was his greatest exemplar. Will's legal practice was flourishing, enabling him to invest in rental properties, but also requiring the addition of an associate. So he invited a young lawyer from Iowa to join the firm and, especially, to handle the court work since Jameson was having problems with his hearing. He had led a busy life since coming to Roundup in 1908, getting thoroughly involved in the town's development. He conducted the census and helped push through the city's incorporation, and then served as city clerk and attorney. He was on the committee which secured the creation of Musselshell County on March 2, 1911. He helped to organize the volunteer fire department.

Will had a particular interest in education, reflecting his personal commitment to learning and the hard road he had had to follow. He served on the school board from 1910 to 1913 and helped to win accreditation for the high school by the time the first class graduated in 1914. He supervised the organization of the Keene Coal Mining Company and was active in land development and management in the Roundup region. In March, 1912 his old friend, now Federal Judge George M. Bourquin, named him as U.S. Commissioner. His fees as the homesteaders flocked in were a profitable addition to his legal practice. One post which he declined was that of mayor of the town. He was a delegate to several Republican state conventions, but did not pursue elective office on the larger scene.

Politics did figure prominently in family conversations, and, especially, as the Election of 1912 came around. Will was a great admirer of ex-President Roosevelt, but he did not think that "Teddy" should split the party and risk putting a Democrat in the White House. So he stayed with President Taft, who came in third in that memorable race. And Woodrow Wilson, as he feared, took up the mantle of high office. Jameson was also active in the Roundup Commercial Club and in the Masons.

May of 1915 found Willie and his classmates anticipating commencement later that month. On the 7th, however, word was flashed across the Atlantic of the sinking of the *Lusitania*, bringing Europe's conflagration tragically closer to the Roundups of the land. The Cunard liner, Britain's fastest, proudest merchant ship, was torpedoed by a German U-boat without the conventional warning off the Irish coast, on the last leg of her voyage to Liverpool. The *Lusitania* went down in eighteen minutes, with 1,198 lives lost, including 128 Americans. Shock and anger echoed the catastrophe, though it was mostly in the eastern press that emotions flared into talk of war. Places like Butte and Roundup were far too diverse in nationalities to offer one view.

Commencement week began on Sunday, the 16th, with the baccalaureate service at the Star Theater. Class night exercises came on Thursday and then commencement the following evening. Six young men and seven young women composed the second class to graduate from Roundup High. Willie was president and headed for a distinguished career in his chosen profession of the law. Seymour Gorsline was vice-president and would later become city editor of the *Los Angeles Times*. Carl Knudsen, secretary, would enter the Congregational ministry, while Harry Griffin, treasurer, would also choose journalism and serve for a while as an editor of the *Billings Gazette*. Josephine Sutherland and her colleagues had taught them and their classmates well, better than they knew and had put real meaning into the class motto: "Not for school but for life, we learn."

Not long after commencement, Will's too-busy life caught up with him and he suffered a crippling stroke. Thereafter he would walk with a limp and carry a cane. Since Willie would be going to the university in the fall, it was decided that the family should move to Missoula where the elder Jameson could take life easier and recover his health. Income from the rental properties could help the family keep going. Meanwhile, he went to Butte for medical treatment and Willie enrolled in the Butte Business College and spent the summer learning how to type. There was an emptiness in Grandmother Charity's home with Philip's passing the year before, and she was glad to have father and son with her. That left Annie with the burden of the move to Missoula. It was a time in her life, daughter Lucille later recalled, when her mother no longer sang.

CHAPTER THREE

PREPARATIONS AND BEGINNINGS

If Will's illness ended the Roundup years and signalled uncertainty about the future, the family nonetheless found hope in the move to Missoula. Bill's education (he dropped "Willie" halfway through high school) was an important consideration, but, perhaps, the elder Jameson would recover his health and be able to resume the practice of law. If not, there was his second love, building houses, and in the rapidly growing community of Missoula (from 4,366 in 1900 to 12,869 in 1910) there would be ample opportunity to apply his skills. Income from rental properties in Roundup would help, but Bill and Lucille would have to find part-time jobs for their spending money. He would be staying at home, but otherwise would have to earn his way through college.

They moved in August, 1915 to a house on Eddy Avenue, not far from the campus. "Old Marion" had been sold, but there were streetcars to meet the family's transportation needs. Missoulians were feeling good about their progressive town. Life was pleasant in most respects in this beautiful, well-watered valley, with its protective mountains moderating winter's cold and summer's heat-laden winds. "Whatever natural advantages have done for Missoula," a chamber of commerce publication pointed out, "its citizens have done more.... Missoula is a town of handsome

Home on Eddy Avenue, Missoula

buildings, pretty residences and wide, clean streets. Missoula is one of the cleanest cities in the United States, physically and morally. It is not the province of a description such as this to enter into sociological discussion, but that the 'lid' is ever on in Missoula may be casually mentioned, perhaps without offense."[1]

The new University, of course, figured prominently in the town's view of itself and of the future. Leading citizens had gone to Helena in 1893 to lobby legislators with both argument and well-lubricated entertainment for a Missoula location for the proposed university. Despite Paris Gibson's generous offer of land and money for a single unit in Great Falls, the Missoula men were successful in landing one of four sites. Advice sought from educators around the country strongly favored one unit, but political considerations saddled the new state with the more costly alternative. Bozeman, Butte, and Dillon also got a piece of the pie.[2]

The University opened in September of 1895 in the old Willard School on the corner of West Sixth and Ash Streets. It wasn't much of a beginning, offering schooling on a shoestring, but a crowd of 300 gathered on the 11th to hear speakers dwell upon a future bright with promise. Col. Wilbur F. Sanders, that veteran of many new beginnings in Montana, urged that this become a place where love of learning would "be pursued as a bride." "The

State," he admonished the assembled citizenry, "confers upon you a high responsibility and a most solemn duty."[3] There were fifty students at the outset, only five of whom were prepared for college work. For the next ten years, the majority of entrants studied in a Preparatory School before being admitted to college-level learning. By 1908, however, there were 28 accredited high schools in Montana and the preparatory department was discontinued.

First president, Dr. Oscar J. Craig, was a good organizer and versatile educator with an optimistic temper requisite for the job. A faculty of five ranged widely over the various fields of study, with Craig himself teaching history, philosophy, psychology, literature, and political science in addition to his administrative responsibilities. He served until 1908 and saw the institution well established on its own spacious campus. The capable Craig was followed by the brief presidencies of Dr. Clyde A. Duniway (1908-1912) and Dr. Edwin B. Craighead (1912-1915). Both men were able educators but inclined to move too fast for their Montana constituencies.[4] By 1915, the year of Bill Jameson's enrollment, there were approximately 650 Montanans and 120 out-of-staters in the University.

II.

Bill preferred the smaller campus scene and liked what he had heard and read about the school in Missoula. During his senior year, the University's Dr. Joseph A. Underwood had visited Roundup and made a strong impression on young Jameson. His power of intellect was a bit disturbing to the smug complacency of the graduating senior. Gently, it seems, this scholarly professor had a way of helping young people think honestly about themselves, rather than just rearranging their prejudices. Underwood was the kind of man and teacher around whom a quality institution could be built. Bill also had examined school publications. In one entitled "What the University of Montana Has For You," several pages were devoted to the advantages of the smaller institutions, along with emphasis on a sound curriculum, strong faculty, expanding physical plant, active social life, availability of scholarships and jobs—all in a beautiful setting! It seemed the right place for the slender young man, just turned 17 and still growing, to top his father by several inches in height.

That first semester he included a course in shorthand, for which academic credit was then given, to go along with his typing skills and qualify him for part-time clerical work in the University. His first job was operating the mimeo and multigraph machines, but he graduated to other responsibilities in the business office and eventually served as secretary to three presidents! Meanwhile, he also became acquainted with janitorial duties on campus in an effort to make ends meet.

A state oratorical and debate league had been formed in 1904 with participation of the other units, and Bill early became involved and would be a mainstay of the University's program throughout college and law school. During his freshman year, however, he was the only entering student to be selected for the "Authentic Society." Prof. A.W.L. Bray, better known on campus as "Archie," had come to Missoula from Cambridge University in 1914 to teach biology. He was instrumental in organizing some of the more "high-powered" students to meet monthly for the hearing and discussing of papers. The topics tended to center in the sciences, though the main theme for 1915 was the major religions of the world.[5]

In the membership of 15 to 20, there were students like Harold Urey who would win a Nobel Prize in 1934 for his work in Chemistry. Others included Howard Johnson, Payne Templeton, and Merle C. "Mike" Gallagher. Howard would become Chief Justice of the Montana Supreme Court, while Payne and Mike would pursue distinguished careers in Montana public education. The first year participants were limited to upperclassmen, but then in 1915 it was decided to pull in any promising freshmen. Bill was selected.

Beyond the sharing of intellectual interests, a strong bond of friendship began to build, with one result that several members resolved to form another Greek fraternity, Alpha Delta Alpha, to go with the three already on campus. Organization occurred in February of 1915, and during "fraternity rush" the following September Bill was one of three pledges from Roundup. The other two were his high school classmates, Seymour Gorsline and Harry Griffin, who were living with the Jamesons at their mothers' requests.

Active in the formation of Alpha Delta Alpha was a long-limbed sophomore who would become one of Bill's lifelong friends. Mike Gallagher was a Congregational minister's son from Wahpeton, North Dakota. When his father decided to uproot for a homestead and a preaching station at Stevensville, Mike had found himself, at 14, in an "immigrant car" with all the family belongings enroute from Wahpeton on Christmas Eve, 1912 to Missoula, where he arrived on New Year's Eve! With temperatures dropping to 30 below, it was a holiday season he would never forget!

Subsequently, the elder Gallagher accepted a preaching post in Missoula and Mike entered the university in the fall of 1914. His father felt that he was Rhodes Scholar material and, accordingly, wanted him well prepared in the classics. So he had Mike register for 5 hours of Greek, 5 hours of Latin, along with 3 hours of Freshman English, 3 hours of Algebra, and P.E. William "Daddy" Aber had been brought from Harvard in 1895 to handle Greek and Latin studies which, however, did not have many takers in Missoula. In fact, Mike was the only student in Greek and had but two girls with him in Latin composition. Risking parental displeasure, he dropped the Greek in favor of 5 hours of Chemistry, which was to be his major interest. Happily, "Daddy" Aber was more popular on campus than his subjects, as evidenced by the naming of the annual clean-up day at the University as "Aber Day"!

In addition to being fraternity brothers, Bill and Mike shared some common enterprises. For instance, in the summer of 1917 they agreed to operate the YMCA store. Though there was no campus store at that time to provide competition, there were limited prospects of making much money. And there was always the danger of two hungry proprietors eating up the profits! Fortunately, Mike was contacted about a tutoring job at Boulder which promised $60 for the summer with room and board. Then Bill was approached about tutoring William Andrews Clark's grandson in Latin. In his view, that would mean taking "tainted" money, a concern of conscience Mike did not share, and since this assignment involved only one student and one subject, he accepted in Jameson's place and spent the summer living in the midst of plenty at Salmon Lake! Bill stayed on campus and worked in the university's business office.

Other friends of his Missoula years included Dave Manning, who would have the longest legislative career in the country, Ronald S. Kain, whose achievements in journalism and writing would bring posts of national and international importance, and Otis O. Benson, Jr., who would have a distinguished record of service as an air force physician. In various fields, the little university turned out some impressive graduates in those years, substantiating its claim of having a quality student body that would be a credit to any institution.

Though Bill's main extracurricular interest remained with debate, he did become involved in such other activities as managing the Glee Club. The singers traveled the state in style, in a private Pullman car, giving performances in Great Falls, Big Timber, Billings, Red Lodge, Roundup, and other places. He was not much interested in athletics but could hardly miss the mounting enthusiasm for the football team during the 1915-1916 seasons. That sport had had rather humble beginnings back in 1897 when the team had to practice in a field near the Missoula River and spend part of its time fishing balls out of the water. But now Coach Jerry Nissen had been enticed from Washington State and had engaged in some "strategic recruiting." With stars like Harry Adams, and "Click" Clark, the team was playing big time schools and compiling a winning record. Perhaps, the greatest moment of glory come on Thanksgiving Day, 1915 when Missoula held mighty Syracuse to a 6 to 6 tie!

III.

The house on Eddy Avenue had few quiet times, especially on week ends with Bill's and Lucille's friends coming around. Campus events were talked over and when the mood so suggested there were strains of the "Boola Song" or "At the Foot of Old Mt. Sentinel." Sunday still meant Sunday school at the local Methodist church and Epworth League in the evening. The boys from Roundup, Seymour and Harry, were expected to go along. By the spring of 1916 Will was feeling much improved and anxious to become more active. A place with some land would meet that need, and soon he found a four bedroom house with three acres at the Orchard Homes tracts. The new location was three miles from campus, but the street car ran to within three blocks. That worked out all right, except for those times when Bill had to stay late at the university, missed the last car, and had a long walk home.

Everyone enjoyed the new place, though it meant a return to outside toilets and pumping water for household uses. There was a porch on front, comfortably shaded by leafy trees, to which the bluebirds came back each spring, much to the family's delight. Irrigation ditches watered a sizeable cherry and apple orchard and a large garden plot. Some chicken houses completed the layout of the Orchard Homes place. Will was inexperienced at farming and

Lucille, 1919

Home in Orchard Homes, Missoula

so went strictly by the book, with sufficient success, however, to surprise his more seasoned neighbors. At harvest time, Annie was swamped with canning hundreds of quarts of cherries, apples, vegetables, and chickens. The Jamesons also sold cherries to the Bitter Root Cannery and eggs and chickens to the Florence Hotel.[6]

Will added a few pigs to his farmyard, but was reluctant to take on a cow. When son Bill offered to do the milking, the elder Jameson allowed that no self-respecting cow would keep his hours! Sunday evenings Bill and Lucille were permitted to invite friends for dinner. By that time, Will and Annie had decided that their children had outgrown Epworth League. Those evenings, and other times, became a part of the fond memories of the Missoula years. The food was as delicious as it was plentiful, conversation flowed, while Bill's girl friend, Mildred, played the piano beside an open window and outside, in the trees, the birds trilled their accompaniment.

About the time the Jamesons moved to the Orchard Homes, Grandfather and Grandmother Richards left Butte for Missoula and found a house four blocks away. Rebecca was now in her early 70's and this would be her final move in the long journey from Cardiff to Scranton, to Nevada, and then to the Montana mining frontier. Following her death in 1920, Richards returned to Butte for a while and then came back to Missoula. Charity alone remained of the old generation, staying at the home in Butte, caring for her garden and for two grandchildren who had lost their mother. She would come to Missoula much later, in 1939, to spend her last two years with Annie and Lucille. There she would sing the old hymns, as Annie or Lucille played the piano, quote Scripture, and listen fretfully to the radio as war engulfed her beloved homeland. Memories faded at 87—except somehow those of her youth and particularly of the journey of the "little English bride" to a distant land of new beginnings—now so long ago.

IV.

The European catastrophe finally overtook the country and the campus in the spring of 1917. Up to that time, the university and *The Kaimin* had paid scant attention to world events. Local grievances and issues grabbed the headlines of that student newspaper instead of the ebb and flow of battle on the western front. Then the marauding German U-boats surfaced to sink American shipping and a weary President Woodrow Wilson called the Congress into special session and asked for a declaration of war. On Good Friday, April 6, the Senate responded 82 to 6 while the count in the House was 373 to 50. One of the 50 was the nation's first congresswoman and an early graduate of the university. Jeannette Rankin was as committed to pacificism as she was to feminism and the cause of social justice. Throughout a long lifetime, and faced with another crucial vote in December, 1941, she would not waver.

In Missoula, as war came, the ranks of the student body thinned and the law school would close for a while. Wooden barracks appeared on campus to accommodate the Student Army Training Corps and would remain to provide the first housing for men and for other university purposes. Bill was in the S.A.T.C. and spent the summer of 1918 at the Presidio in San Francisco. That fall the university, like the world at large, faced a foe as implacable as the Kaiser's legions. The Spanish influenza first struck the western front in the summer of 1918 and spread relentlessly as fall came on, hospitalizing 800,000 troops and killing 50,000. Jumping the ocean, it became a world-wide scourge, claiming by various estimates from 10 to 20 million lives. Reaching the United States in September, it raced across the country and was in Montana by late that month. The usual control methods seemed ineffective and in Missoula the university closed down for most of the fall.

That senior year for Bill Jameson was eventful in other ways. He made the acquaintance of a young woman from Billings, a brown-haired, hazel-eyed freshman named Mildred Lore. Up to this time, he had dated quite a bit but had no "steady." Mildred changed that as their relationship developed deep and enduring bonds of affection. He knew that, whatever else the future might hold, this girl with her music and endearing ways would figure very vitally in his life. They became engaged in the spring of 1919.

Another side of his personality, his political nature, surfaced in his election as president of the senior class and also of the student body. The latter responsibility landed him squarely in the center of a controversy that broke over the campus early in 1919. Dr, Louis Levine of the Department of Economics and Sociology had developed an interest in mine taxation and had prepared a series of monographs on the subject, to be published, he thought, by the university. Both President Edward Sisson and Chancellor Edward Elliott had indicated their support of the project, which was

William J. Jameson

critical of state laws that permitted the mining industry to escape paying its fair share of taxes. Later the Chancellor reconsidered, fearing Company (Anaconda) pressure on the upcoming legislature and possible loss of support for the university. He advised Levine that the timing was bad and suggested an indefinite postponement. When the professor proceeded to publish his findings at his own expense, Elliott suspended him.[7]

President Sisson shared the students' disappointment and disbelief. Young Jameson now found himself helping to frame a strong resolution to the Board of Education. The *Butte Miner* for February 11, 1919 carried a story datelined Missoula, February 10, relating that "virtually the entire student body of the State University with only two dissenting votes registered an emphatic protest against the suspension of Dr. Louis Levine from the faculty at a special convocation held here today." The students criticized "indefinite charges" brought against the professor with "no statement as to reasons."

If Levine's suspension brought support and sympathy on campus and in town, over in Butte the *Miner* was quick to come to the chancellor's defense. In a lengthy editorial the following day, that paper vented its indignation that students would interfere in a matter that clearly was none of their concern. Though some older in years, they were no more entitled to meddle in the supervision of their institution than their younger brothers and sisters in the lower public grades. "The parents and guardians of this state," the *Miner* declared, "have delegated supervisory control of the university to certain duly constituted authorities. The duty of these authorities is very plain." If mistakes are made, they are to be corrected by the people; students "have nothing whatsoever to say about it." Rather, it is for the students to confine " themselves to the studies provided for them, enjoying the proper prerogatives of student life," and thus preparing themselves for "good and responsible citizenship." As for the president of the student body, he was left with a reputation of being a radical in certain quarters of his old home town.

News of the suspension rippled across the country, was picked up in the eastern press and brought an investigator from the American Association of University Professors. Pressure built upon the Board of Education, until on April 7th Levine was reinstated with back pay. That action brought relief to Bill in more ways than one. He was also a student assistant in the Department of Economics and Sociology and had been assigned to teach

Levine's class in Money and Banking. That was not his forte and he scrambled to stay ahead of the students. One error he made the first day was to leave time for questions and that left him grasping for some of the answers. Thereafter, he managed to take the full time with his lecture. Levine's reinstatement, then, came as an occasion for additional rejoicing.

V.

Bill's part-time employment culminated in his serving three presidents as secretary, perhaps the most unique accomplishment of his student years.The first was Acting President F.C. Scheuch, who had been at the university from the beginning and who headed it from June, 1915 to September, 1917. Then came Dr. Edward Sisson, 1917 to 1921, followed by Dr. Charles Clapp, 1921 to 1935. During the Sisson years, in the fall of 1919, Bill matriculated in the Law School and began in earnest his preparation for the career he had had in mind from childhood. He also now insisted upon paying for his board at home.

Meanwhile, the family had moved back into town, to a four-bedroom house at 227 South Fourth Street West.Reluctantly, they had left the Orchard Homes place, but the work and all the visitors had gotten to be too much for Annie and she was developing blood pressure problems. Bill and Lucille consoled themselves that they were now within easy walking distance of the campus. The "new" house required extensive repairs and Will's carpentry skills came in handy. On Saturdays Bill helped his father with the high work and the painting. Will purchased the house in 1921, which, with the exception of two years, would remain the Jameson residence until it was sold in 1972.

It was President Duniway who had first urged the organization of a Department of Law back in 1908-09. Montanans, he affirmed repeatedly, should not have to seek legal training out of state. The legislative assembly in its 1911 session agreed and a bill establishing the Law School was signed by the governor. In addition to a legislative appropriation for operations, the new school received a private gift to start its law library.President Duniway faced his most delicate task in resisting pressures to appoint only Montana lawyers to the faculty and to seek for qualified candidates around the land.[8] Appointments like A.N. Whitlock of Kentucky would justify his efforts.

Home at 227 South 4th West, Missoula

Will and Annie Jameson

Law School, University of Montana, 1922

By 1915 the School was enrolling 77 students and in need of a new building. Meanwhile, it had acquired membership in the Association of American Law Schools. Among new faculty added was C.W. Leaphart, with a legal degree from Harvard, and destined to serve as dean from 1919 until his retirement in 1954. During his tenure, the School would win the reputation of being one of the finest in the West. As early as August of 1923, the American Bar Association was rating Missoula "A," along with only 38 other schools in the country.[9] So Bill would benefit from an excellent faculty in a program that was well on its way.

He still kept up his interest in debate, traveling around the state and on one occasion taking on a team from Columbia University. The topic for 1921-22 was the cancellation of war debts, and a timely one in view of emotions being generated between Washington and her recent Allies. The war had changed the country from a debtor to a creditor nation, with the Allies now owing Uncle Sam over 10 billion dollars. Great Britain and the others thought that the ledger should be closed, in view of the fact that they had borne the brunt of the battle, with staggering casualties and devastated towns and countrysides. But the Harding administration (and, later, Coolidge's and Hoover's) saw it otherwise and wanted payment. Jameson's team argued the case for cancellation and their debates drew good audiences around the state, though few Montanans seemed to be excited about the issues involved.

Bill's politics, in line with family traditions, were safely Republican. Only once did he stray from the fold, in the presidential election of 1920. For him, the issue of the country's participation in the League of Nations transcended partisan loyalties. Clearly America belonged in the League. The handsome Republican nominee, Senator Warren G. Harding of Ohio, seemed to wobble in his campaign speeches between isolationists and the more internationally-minded, telling each what they wanted to hear. Unimpressed, and incurring the elder Jameson's displeasure, Bill cast his vote for the Democratic choice, Gov. James M. Cox of Ohio. Will could be forgiving when Harding won in a landslide. Years later, at a testimonial dinner for Jameson in Billings, fellow attorney Horace Davis recalled the incident and figured that Bill was only 99.44% pure! As a matter of fact, in the congressional election of 1918, though he could not yet vote, young Jameson favored the re-election of Thomas Walsh in the senatorial race, while Will supported Republican challenger Oscar Lanstrum of Helena and Annie cast her ballot for Jeannette Rankin.

Bill's choice for governor in 1920 fared much better than did Cox. He strongly supported the Republican nominee, Joseph M. Dixon, who was coming out of political retirement from his ranch on the Flathead. Bill was well acquainted with three of his five daughters as fellow students and appreciated his advocacy of adequate support for the state university system. Its financial situation was more precarious in those years than in later times. Dixon had also a deserved reputation as a man of principles, acquired during years of public service as a county attorney, Montana legislator, member of the U.S. House and then of the U.S Senate. In 1912 he had bolted the Republican Party to sign on with Roosevelt and the Progressive crusade.In fact, he managed T.R.'s national campaign, to the detriment of his own re-election efforts in Montana and he lost out to Thomas J. Walsh.

Dixon had returned to Missoula to edit the *Missoulian* until 1917, when he moved to the Flathead. His Democratic opponent for the governorship in 1920 was another easterner of Quaker background, Burton K. Wheeler, who had been a controversial U.S. District Attorney in Butte during the war years. His regard for civil rights ran afoul of the patriotic frenzy of the times and earned him the title of "Bolshevik Burt." His backing also included the Non-Partisan League which was charged, among other things, with advocating free love. So the campaign became one of the most vicious to date. Dixon had the support of the mining interests and conservatives generally, including some from the Democratic side. Bill attended a rally in Missoula addressed by Henry L. Myers, then Democratic Senator from Montana, where he spoke in support of Dixon and launched a bitter attack on the "radical" Wheeler and the Non-Partisan League.[10]

Dixon won by a large majority but would serve only one term. His promotion of various new taxes, including a metals mine tax, earned him the Company's enmity and he lost in 1924 to a judge from Kalispell, "Honest John" Erickson. Ironically, the mine tax was carried by the voters. Bill had been impressed with Dixon's inaugural address and felt that he was one of the state's strong governors. He would serve on his campaign committee in 1928 when Dixon ran unsuccessfully against Wheeler for a seat in the Senate. Meanwhile, Bill's interest in politics was sharpening and he intended, when the opportunity arose, to make his own try at elective office.

VI.

Toward the end of his final year in the Law School, he was informed by Dean Leaphart of an inquiry from Johnston, Coleman, and Johnston in Billings. William M. Johnston had presided when Bill debated the cancellation of war debts in the "Magic City" earlier that year. He had been impressed and was also interested in Jameson's stenographic skills. Many young lawyers of the day began their careers with secretarial duties in a firm.

The offer from Billings posed a problem for Bill in that he had been assuming that he and his father would open an office in Missoula. That had been Will's thought, though he had said little about it. He was not able to resume legal practice on his own but believed that he could get along with Bill's assistance. Yet, his son's career meant too much to him to let his own hopes get in the way. When Johnston's offer was made known, Will quickly urged his son to take it, noting that he and Mildred wanted to be married and there was more financial security in a firm salary. Getting a new practice off the ground might mean living on a shoestring for a while.

The Billings firm had an excellent reputation and Johnston himself was a prominent public figure and a leader in the Democratic Party. He had served as county attorney, city attorney, in the legislature, and as mayor during the war years. He had helped organize the Yellowstone Bar Association, had been president of the Montana Bar Association during 1910-11, and was active in the American Bar Association. Clearly, the offer had excellent possibilities and so Bill accepted, moving to Billings on July 1, 1922. As it happened, he and Mildred decided to wait one year more, while she taught English, History, and Music at the high school in Judith Gap and he lived at the YMCA and tried to save some money on his monthly salary of $125.00. Fortunately, after two months he was raised to $150.00 and then to $175.00 the following year.

Johnston, Coleman, and Johnston occupied four rooms on the fifth floor of the Electric Building and that first year Bill was assigned Mr. Coleman's office. The oil boom was on and Coleman was spending full time with Standard Oil of California and operating out of a suite in the Securities Building. For the first six months or so, Bill functioned as Mr. Johnston's secretary, taking his dictation. Johnston was a real master when it came to short pleadings and contract documents. He never wasted a word and that experience provided excellent training for the novice in the profession. Bill was also able that year to get into the courtroom and cut his teeth on a few cases as a trial lawyer. Those initial experiences seemed to confirm the direction of his ambition since childhood to follow in his father's footsteps.

Bill enjoyed the "Magic City" from the beginning, noting that its potential for growth was good, with an economy more diversified than Missoula's or Butte's, its politics less captive to dominant interests, a very active Chamber of Commerce, and strong leadership in community life at large. It was a place that seemed to be heading toward greater things. He soon joined the Lions Club and the Masonic Lodge and in other ways began getting his roots down in Mildred's home town. His first two years he was able to pursue his interest in debating, serving as volunteer coach for the Billings High School. His debaters included Russell E. Smith, who would later serve with him as a U.S. district judge for Montana.

The event that both had been waiting for took place on July 28, 1923. The *Billings Gazette* for the following day announced the marriage of Miss Mildred Lore to Mr. William J. Jameson, Jr. It was an evening wedding in the bride's home, with relatives and a few close friends in attendance. Of course, Will, Annie, and

Mildred and Bill, 1923

Lucille had come over from Missoula for the happy moment. Floral arrangements banked an altar, while the Methodist minister presided and music for the occasion included McDowell's "To a Wild Rose" and "Oh, Promise Me." Mildred was attended by Lucille and sister Mary, while her brother Eugene was Bill's best man. The next day the newlyweds left for a two week honeymoon in the Northwest, including visits in Seattle, Portland, Victoria, and Missoula. Awaiting them in Billings was one of the Cohagen apartments on Wyoming Street, where they were to begin a long lifetime together of married happiness.

CHAPTER FOUR

THE WIDENING WAY

By the early 1920's Billings was evidencing some of the promise foreseen by its founders when they pitched their tents by the Yellowstone back in 1882. To be sure, there had not been the fabulous growth pictured by General James S. Brisbin for his "Magic City of the Plains." Still, pioneer citizens like James R. Goss (who had also helped to judge the debate on war debts) could note how far the town had come.Once it had been "desert land" by the U.S. land office's designation. "There wasn't a tree or bush," Goss remembered, "or a flower, or even a bird to chirp within all that portion of the prairie which was to be the future town." [1] Yet, the "alkali flatters," as they were derisively labeled by the good residents of Bozeman and Miles, put down their roots and by 1890 could claim some 800 determined citizens.That number had soared to 10,000 in 1910 and, according to the U.S. census, to 15,100 by 1920.

But the years between wars would bring hard times. Agricultural states like Montana did not recover after the postwar depression to share in the "prosperous twenties." Rather, the economy faltered as farm prices plummeted and homesteaders in droves left the state. In fact, Montana was the only state to lose population during the 1920's. Billings, however, fared somewhat better with its more diversified business interests, as a distribution point, and with the oil and gas activity in the Elk Basin. Its non-union labor and lower wages also tended to attract companies moving into the state. By 1940 the "Magic City" was claiming a population of 23,261 and an assessed valuation of $38,546,921 (up from $30,822,886 in 1920).

Meanwhile, farm foreclosures and other kinds of defaults were constituting a considerable part of Bill Jameson's workload. His travels took him as far afield as Wibaux and Geraldine, with many stops in between. Mostly, his cases involved homesteaders who had walked away from their land, from machinery rusting in the fields, and from unpaid obligations at the bank. Where farmers were struggling to hold on, the banker usually tried to work things out short of foreclosure. Banks themselves were facing perilous times, particularly the little ones that had multiplied with the towns on the homestead frontier. On one occasion, the state superintendent of banks complained that so many of them were going "busted" that he had lost track.[2] By mid-decade more than 200 commercial banks had disappeared in a flood of bankruptcies unparalleled in the nation. In Billings, the Johnston firm was hired to wind up the affairs of the First National Bank which had been closed for a number of years. Matters had evidently become rather protracted, for in opening the proceedings, as Bill later recalled, Judge Bourquin referred to "this venerable receivership that now comes tottering into this judicial forum."

The trip to Geraldine that first year of his practice was an especially memorable one for the young attorney. That town during its time of fond expectations had voted special improvement districts to provide cement sidewalks suitable to an up-to-date appearance. Such planning did not seem amiss in a prosperous little trading center doing better than one million dollars of business annually. Now, however, there were vacant stores on Main Street, the professional people had moved on to larger places, and Geraldine was in default on payments. Jameson's trip began on the Northern Pacific which ran to within one mile of Three Forks. There, at one o'clock in the morning, he had to leg it from the rails into town. After completing his business in Three Forks, he caught the Milwaukee to Harlowton and eventually reached his destination, fully cognizant of why the firm had selected its youngest member for this assignment.

Aside from such trips around the hinterland, Bill handled probate matters and, under the watchful eye of Johnston, developed skills in drafting contracts and pleadings. The firm accepted very few criminal or divorce cases, but once or twice Bill was assigned by the court to provide counsel when the defendant could not afford an attorney. In those days that responsibility was passed around and carried no remuneration. In the court room, he began to cultivate the quiet, easy-going manner and the remarkable memory of detail that would characterize his career as a trial lawyer. In July of 1925 he was made a member of the firm.

His involvement in the wider legal community began early with his election in 1924 as secretary of the Montana Bar Association. The new president, Tom Shea, had an office in the Electric Building and wanted his young attorney friend with the stenographic skills in that Association office. Bill served in that capacity until 1929 and made the acquaintance of just about every lawyer in the state. Among his accomplishments was the collation and publication of previous M.B.A. reports. It was a considerable task, in which he had Mildred's assistance. From the beginning, she took a keen interest in her husband's career and, across the years, would be an invaluable source of encouragement and help. Locally, the Yellowstone Bar Association was routinely headed by its first president, Judge James R. Goss, and Bill never held office there. He did join the American Bar Association in 1926, and he would become president of the Montana Bar Association for 1936-37.

II.

One day in early 1926 the Johnston firm was discussing the desirability of one of its people running for the next Legislative Assembly. Attention around the room focused on the youngest member and Bill was not at all reluctant to consider the possibility. Politics had always figured in family conversations and, also, he had enjoyed elective office at the University. So he filed for a seat in the House. Candidate Jameson made his contribution to the Republican Central Committee and purchased some cards to pass around. In all, his investment amounted to about $35.00! That did not include travel expenses as he made the rounds of the county, visiting such places as Ballatine, Shepherd, Huntley, Worden, and Broadview, as well as covering the bases in Billings.

Radios were still a novelty, so it was strictly a personal campaign. At the rallies, he noticed, the youngsters usually filled the front rows. It became his practice to tell the audience how long he intended to speak and then appoint the children as his timekeepers. That held their attention and also assured his listeners that here was a politician with good terminal facilities. Perhaps the hottest issue of the election was bringing a normal school to Billings. Bill was pledged foursquare to work for it. The only piece of the state institutional pie that Billings had gotten back in 1893 was in a bill providing for an Eastern State Prison in the "Magic City." The provisions of the law were never carried out, although a site was selected and a building constructed.

The Legislative Assembly of 1925 had passed a bill to establish the "Eastern Montana State Normal School," to be located "East of the 110th Meridian." The State Board of Education was empowered to make the site selection or to appoint a commission for that purpose. The city chosen was expected to deed land for the school. The Board, with William M. Johnston as a member, opted for the commission, which decided upon a Billings location. Concerned citizens had already acquired and presented to the state 52 acres of land under the rimrocks, overlooking the city. Yet, everyone knew that a major battle was looming in Helena when the Legislature convened. Not only would there be lobbying from rival towns, but existing units of the university system eyed any such expansion with grave concern. Their own funding seemed shaky at best. A succession of presidents at Missoula had worked hard to have one centralized institution of higher learning there.

Bill was successful in his first bid for elective office and went to the Capitol in January of 1927 as the next to youngest legislator in the House. There he teamed with Senator Ernest T. Eaton of Billings to obtain the desired legislation for the normal school. Eaton was one of the founders of the Billings Polytechnic Institute and a veteran around Helena, having served three terms in the House and now was in his first session in the Senate. The Commercial Club back home was, of course, lending strong support and influence. Its secretary, James Shoemaker, was in town lobbying for the Billings school. Bill cut his legislative teeth tending to the floor work in the House, while Eaton and other interested colleagues paved the way in committees and in the Senate. *The Billings Gazette* would later say of Jameson's role that "his work in presenting the merits of Billings as the place for the school and the need for the normal received high praise from his colleagues and others who were in Helena during the session."[3]

The 1927 Assembly amended the statute defining the University of Montana to include the Eastern Montana State Normal School at Billings and the Northern Agricultural and Manual Training School at Havre. The Legislature also passed an appropriation of $50,000 for Eastern for the first year of the biennium and $70,000 for the second. In addition, the institution's support would come from fees and earnings "and all contributions from public or private bounty."[4] Billings' long awaited school opened on September 12, 1927 occupying space donated by the local school district and rented at other locations. First president L.B. McMullen reported that there were 10 full-time teachers to serve 135 students.

Bill enjoyed his stay in Helena and decided to run again in 1928. This time he was the top vote-getter in the Yellowstone delegation, including the support of two opposing groups. One was identified with the Ku Klux Klan and the other was an anti-Klan organization. The Klan had spread across the country following its rebirth in Georgia in 1915. One Montana historian estimated the organization's strength at about 6,000 members in the state.[5] Bill had publically opposed the Klan, but it was active in Billings as well as in his old home town of Roundup, and especially in school elections. *The Billings Gazette* for September 30, 1923 had carried a full page advertisement beginning: "So much vicious and slanderous misrepresentation has been spoken and published about the purposes and activities of the Ku Klux Klan that this statement is prepared and published by a responsible officer of the Klan so that all who care to know may learn the true facts." There followed a listing of "Cardinal Principles" including "White Supremacy." The Klan's presence in town was further attested, from time to time, by burning crosses on the rims. The movement faded in the early 1930's.

Bill's political activities that fall of 1928 also included serving on the executive committee for Joseph Dixon's senatorial campaign. He had become well acquainted with the former Republican governer during the 1927 legislative session, when they worked together on a bill to provide better financing for the University of Montana. Dixon lost to Wheeler who had the support of many conservatives and the mining interests in addition to labor and most liberals. Particularly galling to Dixon was that both Senators "Young Bob" LaFollette of Wisconsin and George Norris of Nebraska came out to Montana to campaign for Wheeler, for they had common ties in the old Progressive crusade. If Bill was disheartened by Dixon's defeat, he was very pleased to see

Members of House of Representatives from Yellowstone County in 1929 session. From Left to right: B. C. Lillis, Robert Leavens, W. C. Renwick, W. J. Jameson.

Mildred's name as one of the four Republican presidential electors. Over in Missoula, Grandpa Richards was all for Al Smith, but that year he compromised his Democratic vote and cast one of the four votes for Bill's wife! So, all in all, the election of 1928 was a busy and fruitful one for the Jameson household.

The 1929 Legislative Assembly, like the preceding one, was embroiled in a heated controversy over a bill to provide free textbooks for parochial schools. It didn't go anywhere in either session, but it did create a lot of hard feelings. In February the Assembly observed Lincoln's Birthday and Bill was selected as the House member to offer some remarks. For him, "it was Lincoln's practical wisdom, accompanied by his deep humanity that makes him, not only America's most popular hero and one of the world's greatest statesmen, but also a living personality today."[6] From his frontier inheritance, the Great Emancipator had learned the lessons of patience, to weigh matters carefully and not to force decisions. Bill also reflected on how Lincoln's greatness rested upon his thoroughness, his passion to learn, his insistence to know as much as possible about the problems at hand. Then there was that sense of humor honed by his engrained honesty, that balance wheel of sanity, that capacity to laugh at oneself and the things one loves and still to love them. To these qualities Bill added courage and commitment to an overriding cause. What the young legislator admired in Lincoln were also becoming the compass points for his own career!

That session of the Legislature produced an editorial in the *Montana Free Press,* portraying the young legislator from Billings as a tool of the corporate interests. Just ten years before, when he had led the defense of Professor Levine, the *Butte Miner* had branded him as a radical! He seriously doubted that there had been that much change in his politics and felt the *Press* editorial was grossly unfair. At the urging of many friends, he prepared a response for delivery in the House. Two seasoned associates, however, Speaker of the House Ralph Bricker, and Senator Tom Kane of Ravalli County cautioned against it, noting that the press always has the last word. Bill agreed and his rebuttal was filed—probably the only speech he ever wrote that was not delivered!

The Helena experience broadened Bill's acquaintances and sharpened his interest in politics, but he decided against a third term. His law practice was becoming more demanding and, also, there was the matter of finances. Legislators at the time received $10 a day to cover all of their expenses and it was far from adequate. On one trip home he had to borrow $150 at the bank to cover costs. Thereafter, he would limit his involvement to a term on the school board and to campaigning actively for candidates in the Republican Party. His services were especially sought in fund raising and as a speaker.

In the fall of 1930, he went down to Hysham to speak on behalf of his good friend, "Hi" Stoutenberg, who was running for reelection to the Senate and for the House candidate on the Republican ticket. Just about everyone in town was there, including his old fraternity brother, Dave Manning, who was also the Democratic candidate for the House. That was a bit awkward. After the rally, there was a dance and both Bill and Stoutenberg made the mistake of dancing with Mrs. Manning but not with the wife of the Republican candidate. He was a much older man and they figured that she would not want to be waltzed around the floor. But the local folk didn't like it and vented their displeasure by electing Stoutenberg's opponent. Manning, who would serve in the House or Senate continuously from 1931, joked with Bill on a number of occasions that if he ever had any election problems he would invite Bill down to Hysham to speak for his opponent!

Bill's continuing involvement in politics also included lobbying for Eastern Montana Normal in particular and the University of Montana in general. He had observed in Helena that the more conservative Senate, even its more liberal members, had the habit of paring appropriations bills to the bone. So the schools were badly in need of strong supporters. The 1929 Legislative Assembly had referred to the voters at the 1930 election a bond issue of 3 million dollars for construction of facilities at state institutions, including the units of the university system. William M. Johnston was again in a position to help Eastern as state chairman of the campaign to get the issue passed. The voters did approve and Bill was back in Helena for the 1931 session lobbying for the Normal's fair share. The sum of $232,500 was designated for Eastern's first building; however, the bond issue was challenged and declared unconstitutional by the Montana Supreme Court.

The Legislative Assembly in 1933 authorized the application for a loan and grant from the Public Works Administration, which was later approved in the amount of $250,000. Ground was broken for McMullen Hall on May 1, 1935 and the first classes were held in the new building in December of that year. Bill's next lobbying assignment would be for the Montana Automobile Association. Later, he would be chairman of the Montana Railroad Association and represent the railroads in the legislature during a number of sessions. So, while he did not run again for elective office, he would remain close to the political scene and enjoy the friendship of leading figures in public life.

III.

He continued to be especially concerned about the welfare of higher education in the state. Charter Day at the University in 1930 provided an excellent forum for expressing his views. The invitation to speak was, in part, recognition of his services to the alumni association. He had been elected Vice President in 1922 and also served as editor of the new *Montana Alumnus* quarterly. He became president in 1925 and continued in that office for several years. Bill's first thoughts that day were for the students in the audience, as he remembered those occasions as an undergraduate listening to some "old grad" gilding the past or speculating upon a still more glorious future. He promised to avoid such "bunk," or make it as innocuous as possible, and concern himself with the pressing questions of the times.

Foremost was the problem of financing higher education as enrollments were shooting up around the land. The "college contagion," as it was being called, was confronting states like Montana with sobering questions. Should the tax payer be expected to shoulder the burden of more teachers, additional buildings, and all the rest? Should the Montana student who was paying about 15% of his educational costs be asked to invest more? Should access to the colleges be limited to "an aristocracy of brains?" Bill had little use for any solution that denied the democratic ideal of public education. "We still believe firmly that such education is justified both on the basis of the state's interest in the welfare of its individual citizens and on the basis of the return to the State in the form of public service and good citizenship on the part of those for whom it has provided educational advantages." No one should be denied such advantages "because of accident of birth or insufficient wealth."[7]

Rather, part of the answer lay in a more enlightened public opinion. Once Montanans knew that their state was lagging behind other states of the Northwest in support of higher education, he was confident that they would provide the necessary funding. He concluded with a reminder to the students that they had a stake in keeping good public relations, that any pursuit of the "unconventional" should manifestly be in the direction of development and progress. The following June Bill gave the commencement address at Eastern Normal and added to his concerns about adequate funding the need to move into the field of adult education, to recognize the importance of continued learning and the constructive use of leisure time.[8] Interestingly, his graduation speeches included two at his alma mater in Roundup, the first delivered in 1924 to a class now numbering 45!

IV.

In the fall of 1926 the Jamesons were expecting an addition to the family and decided that it was time to abandon apartment living. They found a two-bedroom house on Clark Avenue and managed the $500 down payment with the balance of the $4800 purchase price financed at 8% interest. Mary Lucille joined the family on March 15, 1927. Two months later, an event that thrilled the western world was of more than passing interest to Bill and Mildred. For four months back in the summer of 1923, "Slim" Lindbergh had been in Billings and had lived in an apartment next to Mildred's home. The Lores had watched the shy, young man

Home at 439 Clark Avenue, Billings

come and go, working as a mechanic and, in his spare time, treating the town to his dare-devil tricks, parachuting from a plane that advertised Westover's Garage. He had performed at the Midland Empire Fair in the fall and then moved on to Missouri to enter pilot training.

Now, suddenly, he was the "Lone Eagle," still an unassuming, lanky kid but one who had flown nonstop to Paris, giving the 1920's the hero it so desperately needed. Spontaneously they acclaimed him, both the wildly-cheering Frenchmen at Le Bourget, crowding around the frail "Spirit of St. Louis," and a nation back home grown accustomed to business or pleasure as usual now stirred to its soul by high adventure. No one questioned President Coolidge's action in sending a cruiser to bring him back, least of all the proud citizens of Billings. *The Gazette*, perhaps, said it for all: "To the young American it was seemingly merely the achievement of an ambition. To Paris, to France, to America, to the world, his landing Saturday night made him the greatest of heroes mankind has produced since air became a means of travel."[9] Later that year, while flying across the country, Lindbergh went out of his way to drop a message to Billings. In Butte he was given a testimonial dinner and Bill drove over for the memorable occasion.

Mary Lucille and her parents

Bill, 1930

Grandpa Richards and Mary Lucille, 1927

Grandpa Jameson and Mary Lucille, 1929

Several days before the Lindbergh news exploded in the headlines, *The Gazette* carried another front-page item of considerable interest to the Jamesons. Mike Gallagher had been appointed principal of the high school, one of the youngest such adminstrators in the state. Bill and Mildred, with infant Mary Lucille in her arms, met the train when Mike and wife Edna came to town. They breakfasted together and talked over old times in Missoula. Two years later, Mike would go to Great Falls as superintendent of schools but then return to Billings in that role in 1937, where he and Eddie would spend all their years to come

On June 8, 1930 a son was born who would carry the name of William James Jameson into the fourth generation. That year proved to be an especially eventful one for the family. Lucille married and moved to Missouri. Bill and Mary Lucille attended the wedding in Missoula, where she served proudly as the flower girl. Lucille's departure prompted Will and Annie to rent their house and go to Billings. Will had kept up his carpentry activity and had built some houses in Missoula. So he was all primed to tackle a construction project on property Bill had bought at the corner of Avenue B and First Street West. Mildred's father, George Lore, was likewise handy with tools, and the two grandfathers had a good time building both a two-bedroom house and a duplex.

Mary Lucille, now in her fourth year, was impressed with Grandfather Jameson's distinguished appearance, the large, graying mustache, the cane, the dark suits, the quiet, kindly ways that

Mildred, Mary and Bill, 1932

drew children to him. He had a knack for making them feel important. How natural it seemed that he should be the one to feed Billy at the table. Then there was Grandma Jameson, not often without a smile, knowing what to do about a little girl's ailments. With her magical "brow stuff" (a cologne labeled "April Violets"), she could somehow soothe away headaches and the like. Being together that year was a special time for Will and Annie and their grandchildren.

The Lores moved into the duplex, and with two sets of grand-

Mary and Bill at East Rosebud Lake, 1933

parents and an infant, Mildred had her hands full. Fortunately, her volunteer job as organist at the Methodist Church afforded an opportunity to get away from time to time as well as to indulge her love of music. George and Catherine Lore had lived in Pawnee City, Nebraska, where he had held a county office before their move to Billings in 1916. For a while he engaged in selling grain and then took a job as a school custodian. It was always a treat, during the summer vacations, for Mary Lucille to go with her grandfather to see where he worked and what he did. Later, brother Billy would recall that nobody could make a willow whistle like Grandfather Lore.

Lucille's marriage did not work out and she moved to Palo Alto, California to take a position at Menlo School and Junior College. Will and Annie decided to join their daughter in the university town. They enjoyed their time there, going for long walks, comparing the different styles of architecture, and every few days getting an armload of books at the library. Will attended the Masonic Lodge meetings and went to the ball games, while Annie made friends at the church and joined in circle activities. Occasionally, Lucille and her parents would spend a weekend sightseeing in San Francisco, where their old friends of Roundup days, the Knudsens, lived.

By 1932 the Great Depression was laying a particularly heavy hand on the private schools and Lucille felt that she would be more secure back in Missoula working at her alma mater, where she had graduated with a major in History ten years before. She returned to her position as Assistant Registrar and then later became secretary to seven presidents and five acting presidents before retiring in 1964. Their house had been rather abused by the tenant and there was much cleaning and repairing to be done, which kept them busy for some while. Will's health became a problem once more when he developed a hernia requiring surgery. Post-operative infection complicated his condition and Annie was never far from his bedside. Their closeness showed most the night he died. He was delirious, but when he seemed too troubled, Annie would comfort him with—"I'm here, Will"— and that would settle him for a while.

Death came at 68 on September 29, 1933. Letters poured in from Butte and Roundup, touching testimonials of affection deeply felt and of esteem for one who had held to the path of honesty and integrity. Typical of the correspondence was one which read: "I want you to know that I always felt that Mr. Jameson was one of those men who make the world a better place just by living in it, and I have for him a feeling of great respect and love. In a sense such a person can never really be gone because his spirit—the spirit of love and understanding which I always felt in your home—will remain with us always."

That legacy of a close and nurturing home life was uppermost in Bill's thoughts when he wrote in one of his frequent letters of comfort to his mother: "We certainly have the memory of a most happy family, and one we'll have to carry on." He eased her financial worries by assuming the loan on the Roundup property and then, later, sent a monthly check to help with the expenses when Grandmother Charity moved to Missoula. Annie found solace in her faith and in her church, continuing with her third grade class of boys in the Methodist Sunday School. Over the years she had touched so many young lives with a spirit of deep caring, and at least one of her "boys," Carl Knudsen of Roundup days, credited Annie with his decision to enter the Christian ministry.

Aside from her Sunday School classes, Annie had had a lifelong habit of calling on the sick and elderly. Often she visited an ailing neighbor who lived in an upstairs apartment across the alley, taking in dinner for the woman and staying to do the dishes. Such acts of kindness were only outward expressions of a spiritual life that was sustained by daily Bible reading and prayer. Annie also found comfort in her loneliness in the frequent letters from Billings, recounting in detail the doings of the young Jamesons. Notes from "So-So," Billy's name for his sister, and scribblings from Billy were especially welcome in Missoula.

Then, as the children got older, they were permitted to take the train for an extended visit with Grandma and Aunt Lucille. Such times were made memorable by Annie's gift of story telling, relating the old days in "wild Butte," how the hearses raced back to town from the cemetery after a burial, of how Grandfather Will had carried a derringer in his pocket and a 38 Smith & Wesson revolver in his boot during the tense times of Heinze's defiance of the Amalgamated. Her stories were always sprinkled with a lively humor that made them doubly entertaining.

On wash day Annie still relied on her old-fashioned, hand-cranked wringer and tub with plunger. Turning that handle until muscles ached would remain among the memories of her young visitors. Then there were the cherry trees in the back yard and Annie's additional gift of rendering the fruit as delicious pies and tarts. Also, there was her version of Irish potatoes so palatable to appetites young and old. Thus, the trips to Missoula were always full of anticipation. And the years after Will's passing were not for Annie without their compensating joys and blessings.

V.

From his parents Bill had a valuable legacy, qualities of character like courage and patience, compassion and diligence for the work at hand. Like his father, he also had a gentle way with children that drew them to him. Clearly, the young lawyer was the domestic type, who thoroughly enjoyed his family. His letters over the years to his mother were evidence enough of that. Yet, there were the growing demands of his practice that took him away for days at a time. At home he often discussed his work as though the children were adults. So they were introduced early to legal terminology and learned to understand when Daddy was preoccupied. Mary Lucille would remember that day when he took her for a sled-ride, got to talking shop with another lawyer, and walked for a block and a half before discovering that she had fallen off!

She was a serious-minded girl, impressed with life's responsibilities and, particularly, her role in taking care of her brother. Her chief complaint was that he hoarded his allowance and never seemed to have any money for candy or the movies, leaving her to pick up the tab! Billy was hardly appreciative of Mary Lucille's solicitude and threatened to "clean up" on her as soon as he was able. One evening a talkative and confidential Billy advised his father that "So-So" was luckier than he was because she had a brother and he just had a sister! His exuberance sometimes breached the outer bounds of patience and then it was often Mildred who might have to apply a spank. On one such occasion, when she caught him up for discipline, the five-year old exclaimed: "Ah, why don't you kiss me instead!" Mary Lucille could usually be kept in line by a disapproving look from her father.

Church and Sunday School were an integral part of the weekly routine. Bill kept his mother posted on the children's activities in seasonal pageants and programs of various kinds. One letter in late 1935 expressed a tongue-in-cheek concern: "I'm afraid we've been neglecting Bill's religion. Yesterday he brought his Bible . . . to Mildred and wanted her to find where it said 'Give us our *navy bread*'!" Mary Lucille often tagged along when her mother practiced at the church or visited in the parsonage. The minister's wife had health problems and watching the family care for her strongly influenced Mary Lucille in the direction of nursing. Even as a four-year old, she was sure of her life's calling and had her own nurse's outfit patterned after those worn in the Deaconess Hospital.

Christmas of 1934 brought both disappointment and, for the children, unexpected joy. The family had been hoping that Grandma and Aunt Lucille could be with them for the holidays. Unhappily, they could not come, but Christmas morning did produce a little cocker spaniel as an addition to the household. Bill was not really a dog enthusiast, but he could tolerate them and even accept their affection for him. Somehow they preferred his lap. So it was with Carmichael, the offspring of the cocker spaniel and a neighbor's labrador. There was that morning at breakfast just before the family was leaving on an extended trip. Carmichael had to be let out of the basement and taken to the kennel. In his canine way, he knew that it was an occasion for a little affection. Of course, he chose Bill's lap and proceeded to spill his cup of coffee all over him!

By 1936 the family had relocated on Parkhill Drive, first at a place on top of the hill and then in a new, roomy residence they had built at 435. The law firm of Johnston, Coleman & Jameson was kept busy and Bill's family was spared the rigors of the depression. One of Mary Lucille's playmates came from a needy home and tended to be shunned by the other children. The same sense of elemental justice that had led her father to defend the rabbi's son in Butte caused her to befriend this girl. Later, Mary Lucille was outraged when Marian Anderson came to town, thrilled the music-lovers with her incomparable voice, but could not sit down in the railroad depot to have a cup of coffee!

Sometimes on Saturdays the children went to the movies, perhaps with their father to see a comedy like "Popeye the Sailor Man," or with Grandfather Lore to watch the popular child star, Shirley Temple. Or Bill might take his son along while he indulged in a game of golf. Bill Jr. early developed an interest in guns and hunting and more and more, his father gave up golf in order to spend his available leisure time doing what his son preferred. So on a Saturday they would drive to a friend's or a client's ranch and hunt pheasants or rabbits. Sometimes they just practised shooting at old tin cans. That was what they were doing some years later, shooting at cans and collecting pine branches in a wooded area south of Roundup when the news came over the car radio that Pearl Harbor had been attacked. It was Sunday, December 7, 1941.

Though Bill had rather limited time for recreation, he did keep in good physical condition walking the mile and more to work most of the time. Rarely did he take the car. Mildred would drive him to the office when the weather was particularly inclement. Hiking was another outlet for his energies, and that became a weekend routine during the summer after the family had acquired a cabin near Red Lodge. Camp Senia had been started as a dude ranch in the early 1920's. When it became unprofitable, Princeton University used it for two or three summers as a geological camp and then, with taxes and mortgage in arrears, it was boarded up. The Jamesons and two other families were able to buy it in 1937 for a few thousand dollars and then they formed a corporation with additional members. There was a cook to preside at a central dining hall and a camp man to take care of the premises. With the

Painting of cabin at Camp Senia by James M. Haughey

coming of the war, however, the central dining hall was given up and each family built in its own kitchen facilities.

The summers at Camp Senia were all that a child could desire. Mary Lucille was especially appreciative since that seemed to be the only place where she could get relief from hay fever. Just as soon as school was out in June, the families would move to their alpine paradise. There were horses to ride and the long upward trails to Timberline Lake or Mary's Lake. Mary Lucille and the other children also worked diligently on a show to be put on each year at summer's end. Mildred, of course, was enlisted as the pianist, while other mothers helped with making costumes. One particularly memorable performance featured can-can girls. The fathers carpooled from Billings on the weekends, stopping of at Red Lodge for groceries and the latest "funny books." The mothers mildly disapproved of such purchases, but just enough to make it more exciting for the children to get them.

Bill seldom came without his briefcase full of work. But that did not keep him from walking up the trails with the children or, perhaps, getting in some fishing with Billy. Timberline was a preferred spot, a place of particular loveliness, nestled high in the alpine slopes, ready to reward the footsore hiker with the joy of unspoiled beauty. That trail would remain one of Bill's favorites until, in his 60's, Mildred would prevail upon him to take less arduous climbs. Aside from such diversions, there was always the chopping block for exercise, to keep the kitchen stove and the fireplace in business. So, not all his time was spent on what he had brought up from Billings. Yet, it was in the restfulness of this place that the lawyer and, later, the federal judge worked on the cases and the opinions that won him the respect of colleagues around the land. Few places meant more to the Jamesons, with the lengthening memories of the good times spent there.

If Bill brought work to Camp Senia, so most of the family vacations were somehow or other connected with his profession. Mildred succeeded on a very few occasions, like the trip later to Alaska, in getting her husband to leave his briefcase at home. In 1939 the American Bar Association was meeting in San Francisco and that became the occasion for an extended trip the children would always remember. They drove south to Salt Lake City, saw the sights and then went on to Lake Tahoe, to swim in its crystal-clear waters. There was much to visit in the fabled city by the Golden Gate while Bill attended his meetings. Then the route led north to Seattle and a stay with friends, before returning to Billings.

Bill's dedication to his profession and habits of hard work might have made for marital discord if Mildred had not shared so fully in his career. From the beginning, she was both ardent supporter and loving critic, relieving him as much as possible of the minor distractions of daily life, proofreading speeches and papers, frequently traveling with him to meetings. Fortunately, her parents were available to care for the children. There were, to be sure, spaces in their togetherness, for Mildred to enjoy her music and to pursue social and civic interests. But their companionship of spirit and purpose made possible the achievement they both sought.

VI.

Bill's last elective position was on the School Board and he served only one term, from 1930 to 1932. A hot issue of the time reflected the tightening grip of the Great Depression. There was a strong feeling in the community, as elsewhere in the country, that women teachers with working husbands should not be employed, that in view of the hard times, there should be only one wage earner per family. The Board would wrestle with this emotion throughout the decade. Sometimes, when women teachers married, the ceremony became one of the most carefully guarded secrets in town. As a fourth-grader, Mary Lucille witnessed such a wedding and was sworn to keep it quiet, which she did despite some qualms of conscience.

Another provocative topic for the Board was the ban on smoking by women teachers. They were expected not to smoke in public, though the same restrictions did not apply to male teachers. That double standard troubled enough Board members to keep it as a topic for several years. No smoking at all was permitted on the school campus.

Bill would remain active in the Republican Party, raising money for candidates and serving for a while as the party's state treasurer. His appointment to the federal bench would end any partisan activities. He especially enjoyed the campaigning, noting to his mother in a letter of November 1, 1934 that he had made "four political speeches" in the past week. A few days later, with the votes in, he wrote to her again: "Well at least the election is over, even if I do have little to show for my efforts. We did succeed in putting over two of the legislative candidates I induced to run, and altogether have a somewhat better legislative lineup than we had two years ago." In the U.S. Senate race that year, Bill supported his father's old friend from Butte. George M. Bourquin had retired as a federal judge and was running against incumbent Burton K. Wheeler. Bill had the opportunity to introduce Bourquin at a large rally in Billings. The "tough" judge had had a colorful career on the bench, but he did not have a chance to beat Wheeler, who carried every county in the state and was re-elected by an overwhelming majority.[10]

The widening way of involvement in his profession and in the community at large included membership in the Lions Club, the Masonic Lodge, and the Yellowstone Chapter of the American Red Cross. Partners William M. Johnston and Henry Coleman were Rotarians, but Bill opted for the Lions, joining the club in 1923. Lions International was the newest of the main service organizations, having been founded in 1917, with Kiwanis coming two years earlier and Rotary tracing its beginnings to 1905. He became vice-president of Lions in 1924 and that same year was asked to give a speech to Rotary on the history and significance of the service clubs.At that time they were being lampooned by writers and critics like Sinclair Lewis (*Babbit*, 1922) and H.L. Mencken for their conformity to business rule and middle-class values.

Bill researched his topic and defended the service clubs as the logical result of an awakened social consciousness. Rather than being complacent, Rotary, for instance, had taken the lead in developing codes and standards of ethics for the conduct of various businesses and trades. In a word, the service clubs were functioning to humanize the world of commerce, to remind business and professional people of their responsibilities toward their employees, competitors, and patrons. In the young attorney's view, over "a quarter of a million men through these clubs . . . [have been] led to a little higher standard of ethics in their business dealings with their fellows, and to a higher conception of their obligations and responsibilities as citizens."[11] Additionally, the service clubs fostered fellowship, worked to improve their communities, and through their international organizations promoted a spirit of world-wide good will and understanding. Bill repeated his speech for the Lions Club and it was subsequently published in the *Lions Magazine*.

He stepped up to president in 1925, to find the local club's finances in rather bad shape. The former "happy-go-lucky" secretary had said nothing about a $300 debt. That constituted a particular problem in that the new president and his officers had invited the Lions from Wyoming and Montana to hold their district convention in Billings—the first one in the state! A "Housey-Housey" (Bingo) booth at the Midland Empire Fair, conceived out of dire necessity, netted over $600 and the club was once more solvent and in a position to proceed with plans for the district convention. A very significant development of those years was the beginning of the Lions Camp for boys and girls in the Beartooth Mountains outside of Red Lodge. Bill's loyal participation in Lionism would be recognized when he was made District Governor of Montana and Alberta in 1941-42.

He continued with the family tradition in becoming a Mason in 1923 and would serve as Master of Ashtar Lodge in 1929. That year he had the pleasure of conferring the Third Degree on Ernest T. Eaton in Helena during a session of the Legislature. Some thirty years later, he would have the opportunity of presiding at the ceremonies raising Bill, Jr. to Master Mason. That involved relearning all of the ritual, but it was a moment the elder Jameson did not want to miss.

His involvement in the Red Cross, heading the Yellowstone Chapter, was one of his most extensive commitments of time and energy, lasting from 1931 to 1945. Leon Shaw, editor of *The Billings Gazette*, had been chairman and persuaded Bill to assume the role which expanded greatly during depression years. While Billings was not hit as hard as many places, there was still plenty of relief work to be done. About the time Bill was thinking of stepping down, World War II broke out and he continued as chairman for the duration.

In 1929 he was offered a position as general counsel of the Federal Land Bank in Spokane, just doubling his salary, but he declined. Life in Billings was busy but good, rooted in a family he loved, in a profession he enjoyed, in a community and state worth serving, and in the land of his birth where he could feel truly at home.

CHAPTER FIVE

ROAD TO THE A.B.A.

There was precedent in the law firm for participation in bar activity. William M. Johnston had helped to organize the Yellowstone County Bar Association, was president of the state bar during 1909-11, and belonged to the American Bar Association. Henry Coleman was less involved but was active in the county bar. Bill was admitted to the Montana bar in 1922 and, as we have seen, was made its secretary two years later and would serve for the next five years. He joined the A.B.A. in 1926 and attended his first meeting that year in Denver. It was not until 1935, however, that he traveled to another annual assembly in Los Angeles. But the following year would mark a turning point. With his election as president of the Montana Bar Association at its Golden Jubilee Meeting in Bozeman in August of 1936, the 38-year-old attorney would begin his long involvement with the A.B.A.

It was a momentous time for the Association, which dated from 1878. Fewer than twenty per cent of the country's lawyers belonged, with only 2,000 to 3,000 attending annual meetings. The dentists did much better with 10,000 or so at their yearly gatherings, while the American Medical Association could claim in its membership some sixty per cent of the doctors in the country.[1] The A.B.A. operated on a selective principle, requiring five years of practice for eligibility, along with other criteria. Membership when Bill joined in 1926 stood at 24,000 and had increased only to 29,000 by 1936.[2] Critics charged that the Association was not representative of the profession and was overly concerned with internal matters to the neglect of public issues.

Earlier, the plight of the A.B.A. had been addressed by one of the pre-eminent lawyers of the century. Elihu Root had urged the Association to "enlarge its membership, to improve its procedures, to increase its scope and efficacy, to strengthen its authority and its appeal in the real life of our time."[3] So, it was with accumulating concern and after careful study that the A.B.A. undertook a sweeping reorganization in 1936, adopting at its annual meeting a new Constitution and By-Laws. Central in the revised plan was the establishment of a House of Delegates to make the A.B.A. more representative of the legal community throughout the country.

II.

Bill attended the initial meeting of the House of Delegates in January of 1937 in Toledo. That fall he would have the opportunity to explain what was happening within the A.B.A. to the lawyers of Montana and Wyoming. Meanwhile, he was to become involved in an historic controversy over the U.S. Supreme Court. On February 5 President Roosevelt surprised the Congress with six proposals for court reform, including a provision for the addition of as many as six new justices to the high bench. He had been fuming over the Court's disallowance of New Deal legislation (First AAA, NRA) and the narrow interpretation of federal economic powers by the Court's conservative bloc. Since the aging justices gave no indication of retiring, he proposed, in effect, a means of outvoting them.

Opposition formed quickly in the Congress and in the A.B.A. Southern Democrats joined the bulk of Republicans and found a surprising leader in liberal Senator Burton K. Wheeler of Montana. He had had some differences with the President, but nothing approaching an open break. Now he was prepared to risk his political career over the "court-packing" business. Roosevelt's action reminded him of his wartime experiences as U.S. Attorney when he and Judge Bourquin had worked to stem the tide of war hysteria in Montana. He remembered that the "bill of rights remained in force (during the First World War) only because of the existence of an independent judiciary."[4] "If a President," Wheeler would write later, "could make both branches of government subservient, I feared totalitarianism could happen here as well as anywhere else." To Roosevelt's overtures for cooperation, he replied: "The Supreme Court and the Constitution are a religion with a great many people in this country."[5] This master of the legislative game was determined to defeat the court bill, despite growing pressure from home to go along with the President, especially from farm and labor leaders.

Out in Montana, the state bar president found himself enlisted in the cause, at the request of the A.B.A. "I spent a considerable portion of my time that year," Bill later remembered, "in organizing the lawyers in Montana to write Wheeler commending him for his opposistion to the Court plan."[6] Surveys taken by the A.B.A. of both member and nonmember attorneys and one conducted by the Montana bar showed support for four of the President's proposals but strong disapproval of tampering with the high court. For Bill, the episode was the beginning of what developed to be a rather close friendship with Senator Wheeler, although he had actively supported his Republican opposition in gubernatorial and senate races.

In Washington, while Roosevelt cultivated public opinion with his "fireside chats," Wheeler and his cohorts made ready for the crucial hearing before the Senate Judiciary Committee in March. The Supreme Court Justices, including liberals like Louis D. Brandeis, were indignant over charges that they were behind in their work, and Chief Justice Charles Evan Hughes gave Wheeler a written denial. That letter was produced with telling effect at the critical moment in the hearing and the Committee reached an unfavorable recommendation on the bill. Later, it was killed on the Senate floor by an overwhelming vote of 70 to 20. By that time, however, the Court was already evidencing some change in upholding the Wagner and Social Security Acts. Also, several of the older justices were beginning to retire.

The court-packing controversy was still in the air when the Montana and Wyoming Bars met in joint session at Canyon Hotel and Lodge in Yellowstone Park on September 2-4. Bill had had a major role in planning the event, which was probably the high point of his year as president. Speakers scheduled for the convention included President Frederick H. Stinchfield of the A.B.A., the Honorable Willis Van Devanter, just retired from the U.S. Supreme Court, and, from Washington, Senator Wheeler and

Meeting in Yellowstone National Park, 1937

Senator Joseph O'Mahoney of Wyoming. At the last minute, Wheeler of Montana had to cancel and was replaced by Chief Justice John W. Kephart of the Pennsylvania Supreme Court. He was vacationing at a ranch near Livingston and responded with an address on "The Lawyer."

Interest naturally focused on Mr. Justice Van Devanter who had retired in June. He had been appointed by President Taft back in 1910 and, in point of service, was the senior justice and a highly respected member of the conservative bloc. Wyoming was home though he had been born in Indiana. Here he had practiced law, served as chief justice during the territorial days, and hunted with Colonel Cody. His listeners were disappointed if they expected some reflections on the late unpleasantness in Washington. That, he observed, would be inappropriate as he proceeded to comment in general terms about the workings of the high court, mentioning some of his colleagues, and then talking about the trip which he and his sister had just made to Russia and Germany.

There was one story, however, that was a kind of a postscript to the court-packing episode. Van Devanter recalled a writer who had prepared a very negative biography of George Washington. He took a copy to President Coolidge, who had already seen it. When he asked him for his opinion, the President walked to a window looking out on the south expanse of the White House and to the Washington Monument beyond. "I came over here when I finished [your book], and I looked out there and I saw the Washington monument, and I saw that its foundations were not disturbed, and it was standing there as a mark by the American people to the greatest man that ever lived in America." Likewise, the Justice doubted that the foundations underlying the Supreme Court had been disturbed.[7]

Van Devanter was a very personable individual who loved to visit. He had lost his wife a few months earlier and was accompanied to Canyon by his sister. Her chief function was to try to get the Justice to bed at a reasonable hour. One night at around 1:00 A.M. she enlisted Bill's help in trying to locate him. They found him in a secluded corner of the old Canyon Hotel reminiscing with pioneer Judge O.F. Goddard of Billings.

The meeting at Canyon was the Fifty-First for the Montana Bar and, also, the 150th anniversary of the framing of the American Constitution. Several speakers reflected upon the accomplishments of the founding fathers, while two made reference to the new constitution of the Soviet Union. President Stinchfield was particularly complimentary in his remarks, noting that the two-day convention was better than anything the A.B.A. put together for its annual meetings. He could not refrain from some mention of the court-packing episode and was high in praise of Montana's Wheeler and Wyoming's O'Mahoney—though "I'm not sure that either gentleman will be grateful for praise given in a conservative convention."[8]

In his presidential address, Bill turned to the topic of the recently created House of Delegates. He had come away from the January meeting in Toledo "impressed with the fact that this new organization presents a medium through which the American Bar Association and the various state and local associations may cooperate and correlate their work in more effective service both to the legal profession and to the public."[9] The 166-member House was composed of state delegates (elected by A.B.A. members in the state or territory), state bar association delegates, local bar association delegates, Assembly delegates, chairmen of the various A.B.A. sections, officers of the A.B.A. and affiliated organizations, and the Attorney-General and Solicitor-General of the United States. Thus constituted, the House was representative of the legal profession as a whole, as distinguished from just the A.B.A. membership. Functioning in a policy-making role, the House also elected the Board of Governers, the president and other officers.

The A.B.A. would continue to be criticized for not being representative of the profession and not responsive to public issues. But the reorganization of 1936 did open up the ranks. By the time of Bill's presidency in 1953-54, the Association had over 50,000 members! Equally important, he told his hearers that day at Canyon, there was now "a medium through which the lawyers themselves, in a spirit of public service, may maintain and raise the standards of the profession, remove the unfit and unscrupulous from their own ranks, curtail the practice of law by lay agencies, and cooperate with other organizations and citizens in promoting the better administration of justice."[10]

The joint meeting of the bars was a fitting conclusion for Bill's year in the presidency, one which had seen a notable increase in membership. Equally rewarding was his widening circle of acquaintanceship in the legal profession. It was Mrs. Stinchfield who first suggested to him that he should consider at some time becoming a candidate for the presidency of the A.B.A. In the House of Delegates, Bill would serve in one capacity or another with an outstanding record of faithfulness. Many years later, in an interview in 1975, this member from Montana could recall that he had missed just 3 of 76 meetings![11]

III.

The late 1930's and early 1940's were also eventful years for Bill's law firm. Senior partner W.M. Johnston died in 1938 and two years later, in September, Arthur F. Lamey of Havre joined the firm, which now became Coleman, Jameson and Lamey. Lamey was active in the Democratic Party, would serve as state chairman and head of the Montana delegation to the national convention in 1944. He would be a candidate for governor in the Democratic primary in 1940 and 1948 and later serve on the President's Advisory Committee on Civil Rights and as a member of the U.S. Delegation to the United Nations in 1960. In addition to Lamey, the firm included Cale Crowley from Butte and James H. Kilbourne of Helena. Earlier that year, in March of 1940, the firm was appointed Division Counsel for the Northern Pacific Railway

Company. So Suite 516 in the Electric Building housed a growing legal practice.

Bill's day, with his prodigious appetite for work, began at 7:30 A.M. and usually lasted well into the evening hours. He still covered the concerns of a general practice but particularly enjoyed the encounters of the trial lawyer. Somewhere back in the levels of awareness was the small boy in Roundup waiting for the judge from Billings or Lewistown to come to town so he could see attorneys at work in the courtroom. Cale Crowley, who joined the firm in 1936, found Bill to be "one of the ablest trial lawyers I have ever seen . . . quiet, easy-going, never tyrannical or spectacular . . . always on friendly terms with the opposition, the witness, the court and the jury. He's one of my ideals of a trial lawyer."[12]

Along with the warm and friendly voice and mannerisms went a sharp mind and remarkable memory. Little missed barrister Jameson's attention as he researched a case. There was, Crowley remembered, the case of the Catholic girl, her Butte attorney, and the jury foreman whose name was Kelly. The attorney gave the foreman his sole attention, appealing to the plaintiff's faith "in its most Hibernian aspects." Far from protesting such blatant pandering to prejudice and emotion, Bill "smoothly abetted the performance, and the opposing lawyer relaxed in triumph as the jury took over the case. The verdict, however, went against him." "What the hell kind of Irishman was Kelly," he sputtered. Jameson had researched that question and knew precisely what kind of Irishman headed the jury. "He wasn't Kelly at all, he was Kelley, of stout North Irish Protestant stock."[13]

Throughout his career as lawyer and as federal judge, Bill's colleagues marveled at his ability to cite name, number, date, and substance of cases he had tried long before. It was a faculty, constantly reinforced with usage, which would not desert him with the advancing years. Much later, an impressed law clerk would witness the Senior Judge's memory and careful attention to details at work during a complicated case on appeal in Seattle. " The transcript of the lower court proceedings was voluminous," he later recalled. "During appellate counsel's opening statement of the facts the Judge interrupted to clarify what he believed was a misstatement by counsel in light of the transcript. The attorney, completely familiar with the case, stated the Judge was in error and that the facts were precisely as he had stated."

No one in the courtroom doubted the attorney's statement, but while he was continuing with his presentation of facts, the Judge quietly thumbed through several hundred pages of transcript until he found what he wanted and brought the item to the attorney's attention. Dismayed, he turned to the page indicated, read it to himself and then admitted that he was in error. That case, the law clerk remembered, was only one of three difficult cases argued that morning and one of a dozen or so the Judge had before him that week. "He was equally prepared for all of them."[14]

Bill's practice as a trial lawyer took him into various courtrooms in the state, and there was one judge who particularly impressed him. Charles N. Pray's career in law and politics began shortly after statehood. A Yankee from Vermont, he narrowly missed appointment to the Naval Academy at Annapolis before going to Chicago, where he tried journalism and the theater before settling on the law. The lure of the West landed him in Fort Benton in 1892, there to establish a legal practice and then, five years later, to become assistant county attorney. Then followed four consecutive terms as county attorney in what was then the largest county (Chouteau) in the nation. That time provided plenty of frontier adventure, fighting blizzards on the way to try cases, and prosecuting the likes of Kid Curry and his Landusky gang.

In the fall of 1906, at age 38, he was the last to serve as the state's only representative in Congress. There he would join Senators Carter and Dixon in what was also Montana's last all-Republican delegation in Washington. Two pieces of legislation which received his strong support were the bill creating Glacier National Park and the modified homestead bill. In the first, he faced the opposition of the powerful Speaker of the House, "Uncle" Joe Cannon of Illinois, but with the help of his eastern Democratic friends he got the measure passed, while Joseph Dixon was engineering its passage through the Senate. Pray counted the Three-Year Homestead Act, liberalizing the terms of land occupancy, as of great importance. "That law," he would remember, "did more to settle the public land states of the West than anything else."[15] Aside from the legislative accomplishments, Pray would recall with pleasure (and related to Bill) the occasion of President Taft's inaugural ball in 1909. It was one of those very formal affairs with the men wearing full dress. Unfortunately, Joe Dixon did not have suitable attire, nor did John Nance Garner of Texas. So Pray did the noble thing and escorted their wives, along with Mrs. Pray, to the ball. He recollected that it wasn't much of a sacrifice, since all three were very attractive women!

When he was defeated in his bid for re-election in the GOP-

Progressive standoff in 1912, he returned to Montana and joined with Llewellyn L. Callaway in what would become one of Great Falls' leading law partnerships. Politics pulled him once more into the arena when he ran an unsuccessful campaign for the Senate in 1916 against incumbent Henry L. Myers. In September of 1922 Callaway moved up to Chief Justice of the Montana Supreme Court and then, early in 1924, Pray was appointed by President Coolidge to the federal bench. He joined Judge Bourquin who, until that time, had been the only federal judge in Montana. Pray elected to stay in Great Falls and run his court from there, while Bourquin served the western district. Among his closest friends was artist Charlie Russell. They both had cabins on the Flathead. Pray would continue on the bench for 33 years, retiring at age 88! Chief Justice Earl Warren and Associate Justice William O. Douglas were among those praising the judge's outstanding career during the annual conference of the Ninth Judicial Circuit in Glacier Park in July of 1959.

Bill had limited opportunity to know Pray personally, since at that time the judges kept a distance with attorneys, especially when they had cases in their courts. But he was impressed with those traits which he felt befitted the bench: hard work and solid study, integrity and fairness, and a certain modesty and gentleness that only enhanced strength. Later when he succeeded Pray on the federal bench, he would become much better acquainted. Then, whenever Bill was in town holding court, the retired judge insisted on entertaining him, Mildred, and any staff at the country club. Following dinner, the stories would flow—like the time the bootlegger shot up his court. Fortunately, the inebriate's aim was bad and nobody was hurt. "Dear Judge," he confided in a note to Pray, "I have nothing against you at all. You gave me a fair trial and I was satisfied but I'm going to get those prohibition agents and clean up the docket for you so you can go home."[16] A friendly jury, Pray remembered, acquitted the bootlegger of the shooting charges!

IV.

At the time Bill was practicing in Judge Pray's court, he had no particular aspiration to occupy the federal bench. It was a position that called for dedication and integrity, qualities that meant a lot to him, but his career left little time for mapping out the future. His firm's appointment in 1940 as division counsel for the Northern Pacific would involve his becoming chairman of the Montana Railroad Association. That organization was comprised of the five main lines, the Great Northern, the Northern Pacific, the Union Pacific, the Burlington, and the Milwaukee Road, but in Montana the NP was "chairman road" and its counsel headed the Association's board of directors. So Bill had another call upon his time and energies in lobbying the legislature and the Washington delegation on behalf of the railroads. In April of 1955 the Association opened a Helena office and brought John A. Willard from a career in journalism to be director. He and Bill worked closely in developing a legislative outreach and a public relations program for the Association.

During the war years and on into the 1950's Bill, then, had a continuing association with the state's political leaders. Four, in particular, became close personal friends, namely, State Senators Hugo Aronson of Cut Bank, Wesley D'Ewart of Wilsall, Zales Ecton from Gallatin County, and Tom Ross from Blaine County. D'Ewart was a rancher with an eastern education and accent who ran successfully for the 2nd Congressional District in 1946 and would hold that seat for three more terms. Bill served as co-chairman of his finance committee during most of the time he was in Congress. D'Ewart ran against incumbent Senator James E. Murray in 1954 and lost a very close election by fewer than 2,000 votes. Wheeler came out to Montana to speak for the Republican challenger, but it was late in the campaign. It was Bill's opinion, shared by others, that if Wheeler had announced earlier for D'Ewart, he would have defeated Murray.

Zales Ecton was a wheat farmer and rancher who discussed with Bill the advisability of filing for the U.S. Senate in 1946. He reasoned that Wheeler would be defeated in the Democratic primary and that many of the veteran senator's supporters could be won over by the Republican candidate. Bill did not agree, in view of the tremendous majorities that had returned Wheeler to office in 1934 and 1940. But he had lost the support of many veterans for his isolationist views, as well as liberals and labor leaders. Ecton proved to be right as Leif Erickson edged Wheeler by 5,000 votes in the primary and was, in turn, defeated by the Republican contender in the general election. Ecton would have the distinction of being the only popularly elected Republican senator from Montana! In 1952 he ran a bitterly contested race with Mike Mansfield and lost by fewer than 3,000 votes.

D'Ewart and Ecton were frequent visitors in the Jameson home, as was also the colorful Hugo Aronson. A native of Sweden, he had come to this country in 1911, unable to speak English and with just the $25.00 minimum required by immigration law. Forty-one years later, he would be elected Governor of his adopted state, to serve for eight years. Meanwhile, he had ridden the rails across the country, homesteaded, served in the army during World War I, worked in the oil fields, become a successful oil rig operator, owned a trucking firm and a farm, served on the Cut Bank city council and in the Montana Legislature for 14 years.

Aronson never mastered English but that, somehow, only contributed to his appeal. In the early days, while working on a construction crew, the rugged and energetic Swede was carrying two planks, while the other laborers were content with one. Hugo, as was his custom, was on the run, giving his boss some concern that he needed a rest. "Hugo," he said, "I thing you'd better take five." "Take five?" Hugo protested, "Hell, I'm having enough trouble with two."[17]

On those occasions when Aronson was flying out of Billings, he would leave his Cadillac with the Jamesons and tell Bill, Jr. to feel free to use it. Young Bill did not need a second invitation and would keep the big car cleaned and shined. On the rear fenders were the tell-tale "ding-marks" where Hugo had been driving at high speed over gravel roads. Once when he was visiting, Bill was detailing a very heated school campaign and noting what tactics the other side was using and what his side was doing. Bill, Jr., then a high school senior, broke in: "Well, I think that is just as dirty as anything the other side has pulled!" Hugo was somewhat startled but also delighted at this continuing evidence of the well-known Jameson independence of mind.

Aronson's contagious good nature won bipartisan support. His subtle sense of humor rarely offended anyone. One time, as Governor, he quipped that he did not dare go out of the state for fear the Democratic Lieutenant Governer would call a special session of the legislature and impeach him. One of his cherished possessions was a letter from President Eisenhower, which he shared with Bill, sent following a visit to Montana, which said: "It was a privilege for a farm boy from Kansas to walk at the side of a farm boy from Sweden, and that, in itself, is representative of the greatness of America."[18]

Bill's soft spoken ways also characterized his behavior as a lobbyist. In the mounting tensions of legislative sessions, he was noted as much for his mild-mannered, uncontentious ways as he was for his abstention from smoking and drinking, which definitely put him in the minority midst the lobbyists and lawmakers of the time. Only occasionally did some provocation break the Jameson composure, did some unscrupulous tactic or abusive language trigger a bit of emotion. Daughter Mary Lucille recalled a hot day on the way to Red Lodge when a vapor-locked engine got to her father and evoked a not-too-impressive "damn!"

V.

Conversations in the house on Park Hill Road reflected not only Bill's involvement in the world of law and politics but also his continuing participation in civic and service organizations. His contributions to Lionism were recognized in his election as District Governor for Montana and Alberta for 1941-42. That was deeply gratifying, but it added to an already crowded schedule of travel. On March 1 Mildred wrote to Annie and Lucille from Chicago, where they were attending a House of Delegates meeting, that Bill had spent his time on the train from Billings getting some much needed rest and trying to figure out an itinerary to cover his remaining Lions Club visits.

Missoula had been one of his scheduled stops in January, and he had had the world crisis on his mind. The war was going badly for America and her Allies. Everywhere Hitler and the Japanese were smashing ahead on the path of conquest. Bill reminded his hearers in Missoula, and elsewhere in his travels that year, that the safety of the nation depended ultimately upon an intelligent concept of liberty, that that was the ground upon which the battle must be fought and won. Liberty necessarily involved responsibilities and sacrifice, and especially in wartime. "It is only by the way in which we recognize our duties and obligations that we may enjoy the rights and privileges of this great democracy."[19]

War was also the background of his leadership of the county Red Cross program. In March of 1944, he traveled to his birthplace to promote the national campaign and to rally support for the local chapter. He was introduced as a Butte product who has "just drifted away to Billings" but who one day would return. The American Red Cross, Bill explained, was facing the greatest challenge in its history and the need to raise an unprecedented $200,000,000. By charter its services were not optional but were an obligation to be fulfilled. In particular, during wartime, there were

Bill Presents to Governor Sam Ford the deed for land at Eastern Normal School.

mandated responsibilities for service men and their families. "No other agency in the country," he pointed out, "has such responsibility." The American Red Cross was the "long arm of mercy" and a "symbol of humanitarianism" deserving of strong support. "Rather than feel that we are making a sacrifice, we should instead look upon our contributions to the Red Cross and to all war activities as a privilege to serve those men and their families who are making the only sacrifice worthy of the name."[20]

Along with the Lions and the Red Cross, Bill also invested time and effort in the Billings Commercial Club, serving as its president in 1947. Earlier in the decade, he had chaired an important committee, a "brain trust" of 13 prominent business leaders, charged with mapping a future program for the Club. The final report came at a meeting where the collective memories of the hearers spanned the years to the city's early beginnings. Pioneers I.D. O'Donnell and P.B. Moss were there to hear what this new generation of leadership had to say about the future of *their* city.

Bill remembered, as an outsider, how the claims of "Magic City" dwellers to civic achievement and virtue had produced a "mixed feeling of admiration, envy and resentment" in the state. "We looked upon most spokesmen for Billings, and particularly its Commercial Club, much the same as a witness who was testifying in a New England court. His testimony, clearly exaggerated, was not shaken on cross-examination. The Judge finally took a hand and asked the witness, 'Have you told the whole truth in this matter?' 'Yes, Sir, Your Honor,' was the reply. 'I have told the whole truth and I guess just a little mite more.'"[21]

The war was necessarily requiring a certain amount of governmental intervention and regulation, but the report warned against too much political control being projected into the peacetime economy. "We must be ever alert to the danger of extending government intervention and regulation to a state economy and control that will destroy the freedoms of choice and action which we have always cherished." Given the system of free enterprise and the continuing resourcefulness, courage, and moral responsibility evidenced by the pioneer citizens, Billings would continue to prosper from agriculture, reclamation, oil and gas, recreation and tourism, industrial development, commerce and transportation, health and education, and a strong civic spirit. Another committee which Bill chaired explored taxation policy and recommended that the city and state would benefit from a sales tax. On the statewide business scene, he served as a director of the Montana Coal and Iron Company and would be elected to the board of the Montana Power Company in 1951.

VI.

So the patterns of a particularly busy life were woven—of the texture of ambition, devotion to profession and the commonweal, and of an understanding and supportive family. Bill, Jr. remembered that it was an interesting way to grow up—in the home of a prominent citizen and one of the most influential Republicans in the state. Sister Mary Lucille, moving into her teens, was less interested in her father's friends and political associations than in the opposite sex. Bill wrote to his mother: "I'm alternately amused and annoyed with my daughter. She's finally boy crazy and is simply nuts at times. Our chief arguments center around whether she is going to walk home or I'm coming after her late at night." Her particular ecstasy was having a date with the hero on the football team. With the wartime gasoline shortage, it was sometimes a problem for the Jamesons to find the fuel for an out-of-town game.

The old attraction of Camp Senia during the summer was a thing of the past. With her new interest in life, Mary (she dropped Lucille in high school) found more and more reasons to stay in Billings. With typical Jameson energy, she was busy earning Girl Scout badges, participating in Rainbow Girls, in church activities, rolling innumberable Red Cross bandages, along with the social routine. "It's awfully hard at that age," Bill reflected in a note to Missoula, "and I suppose from now on, to keep them from loading up with too much." Towards the end of the war, Mary had become involved in a rather extensive correspondence with the Navy. Her current boy friend's older brother was writing almost daily. "Poor Sos," Bill reported to his mother and sister, "doesn't know what to say in reply. In fact, her correspondence with the Navy is most difficult. There are now five, and all of them serious. She got a picture from one this week, inscribed 'To the sweetest little blond I've ever met. Wherever I go in this war torn world, I'll think of you, Mary. All my love.'" Mary knew that home-sick sailors wanted to think that there was someone special back home. It was a problem, though, trying to be special for so many.

Bill, Jr. was relieved that his sister had finally found other interests than watchdogging him when the parents were away. He remembered all too well the time when they were at a convention in Chicago and he, in a moment of adolescent daring, had come home with a pipe and sack of tobacco, intent upon having his first puff. Watchful Mary had caught him before he had a chance to light up, confiscated the forbidden stuff, and lectured him until he was in tears. Later, Mildred had found the pipe and tobacco in Mary's bureau and extracted from her an account of the episode.

Bill, Jr.'s main hobby continued to be guns. His collection had grown to 16 firearms and 3 bayonets by the mid-forties, including Grandfather Jameson's derringer and 38 Smith & Wesson revolver. It got so the elder Jameson was apologetic about further purchases. With the acquisition at one Christmas of a combination rifle and shotgun, he explained to the folks in Missoula: "It seems foolish to get him another gun, but he's so anxious for it (he had been eyeing it almost daily at Montgomery Wards) we couldn't refuse." In any event, there were plenty of guns from which to choose when Bill and his son went bird hunting around Worden or Hardin or just target-practicing on old tin cans.

So during the 1940's Bill and Mildred watched their children grow into young adulthood. They found considerable satisfaction in their various activities and accomplishments, which they continued to share with Grandmother Jameson and Aunt Lucille. Mary remained certain about a career in nursing. She worked for a while at the Billings Clinic and also as a volunteer at the St. Vincents Hospital. Upon graduation from high school in 1944, she became interested in the University of Minnesota Nursing School

Reception, Marriage of Mary Lucille to Dr. Walker Honaker, 1949

program. That September she and Bill, Jr. accompanied their parents to a meeting in Chicago and she stopped by the campus and enrolled for the winter quarter. Bill thought strongly that his daughter should take the 5-year degree program, but Mary argued that the war was on and nurses were needed badly and she should take the 3-year diploma course.That was what she did, though years later she would regret her decision when she was obliged to return to college.

In Chicago, the family spent a memorable week, staying at the Edgewater Beach Hotel, seeing "Oklahoma," attending a live broadcast, visiting the Field Museum, Art Institute, and Lincoln Park. "The kids enjoyed Chicago thoroughly," Mildred wrote to Missoula, "although both were incredulous that any place could be so dirty and grimy. And why wasn't there any sun? They didn't realize . . . that the skyscrapers shut off the sun from the streets as thoroughly as mountains would."

At the University, on a blind date, Mary met Walker Honaker, an air force medical intern from Denver. Their chance acquaintance ripened into romance and they were married in 1949. The Honakers would return to Billings to practice medicine. Meanwhile, Bill, Jr. had grown tall, topping his father by several inches. Graduating from high school, he chose the elder Jameson's alma mater but not his profession. He received a degree in Mathematics from the University in Missoula in 1952. The United States was bogged down in the Korean War and he was commissioned a lieutenant in the Air Force.

That same commencement his father was honored with a Doctor of Laws degree. The *Kaimen* for June 3, 1952 noted: "Mr. Jameson will receive his honorary degree on the faculty's recognition that his warm interest [in University affairs] has not waned in the 30 years since graduation. He is a trustee of the University-Endowment Foundation and is a life member of the MSU Alumni association of which he was president longer than anyone else—from 1925 to 1928. His willingness to help the University in various ways is shown by his consenting to serve as a trustee of the Stella Duncan Memorial fund."

VII.

Later that month Bill was again at Canyon Hotel and Lodge, this time serving as general chairman for the Yellowstone Park Regional Meeting of the American Bar Association. With that kind of recognition, he was nearing the end of his quest for the A.B.A. presidency. He remembered how his interest in the national association had first been stirred fifteen years earlier when, as president of the Montana Bar, he had attended the initial meeting of the House of Delegates and reported his impressions to his fellow lawyers in this same beautiful resort setting.

Following his year as president, he had continued to serve in the House as a state delegate. Then in April, 1943 in Chicago, he had been nominated to the Board of Governors and elected at the annual meeting in August. That prestigious policy-making body was composed of A.B.A. officers and representatives from ten circuits in the country. The ninth circuit included Arizona, California, Idaho, Montana, Nevada, Oregon, and Washington. Many of the delegates felt that the new man should come from one of the states that had not as yet been represented, with the result that Bill narrowly beat out a rival from California. The Yellowstone County Bar at its annual meeting honored one of their own, and Bill reviewed for his hearers the impact of the war on law and the legal profession.

The suggestion planted by Mrs. Stinchfield at Canyon back in 1937 that he consider the A.B.A. presidency at some time was reinforced by President Joseph W. Henderson of Philadelphia when he stopped off in Billings in 1944. Bill played down any ambitions that may have been stirring when he wrote to his mother: "We had a seven hour visit Saturday from Joe Henderson, president of the American Bar Association. He was passing through by plane. . . . Incidentally, if Joe had his way, Mother's ambitions for her son might be realized in a few years, but I'm convinced myself I've gone as far as I ever will in the Bar Association."

In Atlantic City in 1946, however, he was elected as Assembly delegate and continued in the House. Mildred reflected on the most recent developments in a letter to Missoula on November 10th. "Atlantic City is quite a fabulous place—at least the prices were. But we have an increasingly large number of friends in the Association, which makes it much more enjoyable each year. Bill couldn't even keep out of politics there. He was retiring from the board (three-year term on Board of Governors). His cohorts there were really very sorry to have him go off the board. He was nominated for assembly delegate—four are elected at large by those at the annual meeting. Eight or nine were nominated—all from populous places with many delegates at the meeting. I really didn't see how it was in the cards for him to be elected even though I was really astounded at the number of his enthusiastic friends. They were apparently enthusiastic enough to get their friends to vote for him as he was second, so [he] is still in the House of Delegates."

Bill's committee assignments within the A.B.A. touched most of the bases and included the important Budget Committee and the top-level Committee on Scope and Correlation of Work. He served as chairman of the Budget Committee from 1944-46 and, despite opposition, succeeded in having funds allocated for legal aid. That was not deemed by the traditionalists to be an appropriate Association function, but, later, legal assistance programs for the poor would become a major A.B.A. activity. Bill had the satisfaction of being in at the beginning.

He joined the Committee on Scope and Correlation of Work in 1947 and became its chairman in 1949. The Committee's high-priority assignment was to help clarify the fundamental objects and purposes of the Association. The Committee met in Dallas in April of 1951 to finalize the report which was presented at the 74th Annual Meeting of the A.B.A. in New York that September. The several recommendations reflected the intent of the framers to promote the relevancy of the Association, or, as Elihu Root had put it, to strengthen "its appeal in the real life of our time."

For the A.B.A's long-range objectives, the Committee offered:

1. The preservation of representative government in the United States through a program of public education and understanding of the privileges and responsibilities of American citizenship....

2. The promotion and establishment within the legal profession of organized facilities for the furnishing of legal services to all citizens at a cost within their means....

3. The improvement of the administration of justice through the selection of qualified judges and adherence to effective standards of judicial administration and administrative procedure....

4. The maintenance of high standards of legal education and professional conduct to the end that only those properly qualified so to do shall undertake to perform legal services....

5. The promotion of peace through development of a system of international law consistent with the rights and liberties of American citizens under the Constitution of the United States....

6. The co-ordination and correlation of the activities of the entire organized bar of the United States.[22]

It was the kind of direction that Bill believed in and hoped he could help implement. In 1948 he had yielded to the urgings of friends to run for the A.B.A. presidency. The front-runner that year was Frank Holman of Seattle, an older man and a traditionalist, who also had gotten the jump in lining up state delegates. Consequently, he landed the nomination in Chicago. Bill continued as an Assembly delegate and, by the time of the regional meeting at Canyon, was ready to campaign aggressively for the presidency.

Attorneys came to Yellowstone from 24 states, Canada and Australia for this regional meeting of the A.B.A. held in cooperation with the state bar association of Colorado, Idaho, Montana, Oregon, Utah, and Wyoming. They numbered some 800 in all and took over all of Canyon's facilities for that week beginning June 17th. Speakers included *Time's* and *Life's* Henry R. Luce, who proposed a Hoover-Truman Commission, composed of the best philosophers, theologians, sociologists, lawyers, and other experts, to produce "a philosophy of law and government in relation to the needs of social justice." What the world so desperately needs is order, he declared. "Give us that order which without liberty is a snare and that liberty which without order is a delusion." [23] A

American Bar Association Regional Meeting, Canyon Hotel, Yellowstone National Park, 1952

right conception of law, he advised, was a "master instrument" if there was to be a tolerable peace and hope was to prevail over despair.

The meeting at Canyon was not only a busy and eventful time for Bill, but it also turned out to be a place of destiny for Bill, Jr. He was celebrating graduation from college and his last free time before joining the Air Force in Texas by spending these days with his parents. There he met Sue Randall, daughter of one of the speakers, John D. Randall of Iowa. Apparently, it was love at first sight. The next month, in July, they met again at the Republican National Convention in Chicago, where Bill, Jr. was a sergeant-at-arms and an Ike enthusiast. Mr. Randall was a Taft backer but that was forgiven since he had once more brought Sue along. That fall she and mother traveled to Texas to see Lieut. Jameson and presently an engagement was announced. So the meeting at Canyon had been fortuitous not only for Bill's plans for the presidency but also for Bill, Jr.'s future married happiness!

The remainder of that year Bill cultivated the support of state delegates. In January of 1953, Ike's brother, Edward Eisenhower, a Tacoma attorney, was passing through Billings on his way to Washington and the inaugural. He was greeted by Arthur Lamey, a classmate at the University of Michigan Law School, and he told Lamey that he thought that Bill's chances were excellent for heading the A.B.A.[24] The following month in Chicago, at the Edgewater Beach Hotel, the quest ended with his nomination to the presidency, to be confirmed at the A.B.A. Diamond Jubilee Meeting at Boston in August. Not even the long thoughts of the little boy in Roundup had ever envisioned where he now stood.

Mildred and Bill, 1953

Bill, Jr. and Sue, 1953.

C H A P T E R S I X

AT THE SUMMIT

Not since 1916 had the A.B.A. found a president in the Rocky Mountain West. That year George Sutherland of Utah had headed the Association and had gone on to sit on the U.S. Supreme Court. Billings and the state took due note of the honor that had come to one of their citizens. *The Billings Gazette* for February 25 ran a front-page photo and article headlined: "Jameson Named American Bar Association Head. Billings attorney wins nomination at Midwinter Meet." *The Yellowstone News* for the following day announced: "William J. Jameson of Billings this week received one of the world's loftiest professional honors, presidency of the American Bar Association." At the University, the *Kaimen* for February 25 proudly noted what happened at the midyear meeting of the House of Delegates in Chicago the day before.

Later that year the *Billings Times* would observe that "Jameson's election to the A.B.A. presidency reflects well on Montana as well as upon him," demonstrating that the state's educational institutions are "coming of age." " 'Bill Jameson,' as he is familiarly known, is deserving of all the honors that come his way. As a native Montanan and a product of Montana schools he accepts his honors with the humility evident among big men. Likewise he is gifted with the grace peculiar to the West. He will never be too big,

American Bar Association Officers meeting with President Eisenhower, 1953.

nor too successful, nor too prominent to enjoy having his personal friends call him 'Bill.' "[1]

The law firm in Suite 516 of the Electric Building welcomed the attendant publicity while preparing for a very busy year. With a senior partner to be gone most of the time, there would need to be a considerable closing of the ranks. By 1953, fortunately, several able attorneys had joined the firm. Time and again, Bill would remark around the country that his kind of commitment to the A.B.A. presidency was possible because of the full cooperation of his partners and colleagues back home.

It wasn't long before he was packing a suitcase and traveling to speaking and other engagements. Late May found him in Washington with outgoing President Robert G. Storey and the Board of Governors visiting with President Eisenhower. The A.B.A. was taking that occasion to support the White House's proposal for increases in Congressional salaries. Ike was recommending a $10,000 increase for Congress and the Federal Judges, nearly doubling their salaries of $12,500 (with an expense allowance of $2500). The A.B.A. leaders agreed and thought that the Attorney General should also be authorized to raise the remuneration of U.S. Attorneys, at his discretion, up to $20,000 a year.[2]

The next month Bill returned for another commencement address at Eastern Montana College of Education. He had not lost his old interest in educational issues and took the opportunity to stress the wisdom of a liberal arts foundation for learning and the fallacy of too much specialization. Liberal arts, he pointed out, provided a sound basis for both professional competency and good citizenship, a fact recognized by many employers. There was little to be gained in turning out " uneducated specialists."

In early July, *The Great Falls Tribune* reported that Bill was in Fargo as the principal speaker at the convention banquet of the North Dakota State Bar Association. Then came the annual meeting of the Yellowstone County Bar, during which he was both honored and treated to some of the traditional razzing accompanying the occasion. "Ginger Ale Bill" was described as the "probity and purity" of Billings, and a portion of the program was devoted to him and his firm, beginning with the song:

Up in the morning
Already thinking
Just Bill and Mildred
No smoking or drinking.
Off to the office
At half-past seven
Left there last evenin'
After Eleven . . .
Oh what the hell
It's tough at C.J. & L.

Someone in Jameson's role then answers the phone with "Coleman, Jameson, Lamey, Crowley, Kilbourne, Haughey, Toole, Stotesbury, Goff, Carstensen, Gallagher, and somebody in the back room I haven't met yet, Jameson speaking."[3] Bill thoroughly enjoyed the bantering. Like his father, there was nothing in his nature that made for pomposity. So, with the merriment of that evening fresh in mind, he and Mildred entrained for historic Boston on the 15th—for the formalities and august surroundings of the A.B.A.'s Diamond Jubilee Meeting.

II.

By 1953 the A.B.A. counted 52,000 members, 4,000 of whom had come to Boston. There, as *Life* for September 7 pointed out, "they brought an atmosphere of decorum rare in convention cities as they went about sampling the local sea food, visiting law libraries, touring the landmarks of the American Revolution, which members of their profession are given so much credit for

President William J. Jameson.

starting." The "Cradle of Liberty" was an appropriate place for the A.B.A. to be gathering, with its general theme for the year—"Liberty Under Law." Such was the agenda for change that the meeting was being described as the most notable in the history of the Association.

A.B.A. leaders saw the Diamond Jubilee as the beginning of a new era in the Association's life, to be characterized by less attention to intramural matters and more concern for broad issues of public policy. The old attitude had questioned whether new proposals for public involvement were a proper function of the Association, whose primary purpose, it was maintained, was to serve the members of the legal profession and not society in general. Bill's Budget Committee had encountered that resistance in urging an appropriation for legal aid for the poor in the mid-forties. But the forces for change prevailed in a constitutional amendment of 1949 that opened the door for the A.B.A. "To uphold and defend the Constitution of the United States and maintain representative government; and to apply its knowledge and experience in the field of the law to the promotion of the public good."[4]

Two years earlier, as we have noted, the Association had created at its annual meeting a Standing Committee on Scope and Correlation of Work. This top-level body of five members had been charged with seeking to correlate the complex activities of a much larger A.B.A. and to plan a long-range program of objectives and policies. Approved in 1951, five of the six committee recommendations related to the public good. Clearly, for Bill Jameson and his colleagues on the committee, the lawyer had a role and an investment in their fellow citizens' well-being. President Eisenhower affirmed that view in his message to the Boston meeting, observing "that the role of the lawyer in the daily life of our nation and communities is vital to our democracy," that "the lawyer is the guardian of individual liberties granted under our Constitution and their defense is one of the main objectives" of the Association.[5]

Most of the delegates were ready to oblige their leaders with a lively discussion of such controversial topics of the day as the Bricker Amendment. Senator John W. Bricker of Ohio was a Taft Republican who wanted restrictions on the President's treaty-making powers. He had sponsored a proposed constitutional amendment, requiring, among other provisions, House and Senate approval of Executive Agreements. President Eisenhower protested that the rapidly developing nature of international crises called for more Presidential discretion, not less, and his view was argued by Secretary of State John Foster Dulles at Boston. The eminent international lawyer pointed out that there had been no abuse of the Presidential treaty-making power. He was supported by an Association study committee on the Bricker Amendment, which brought in an adverse report. After two days of discussion, however, the delegates voted almost four to one in favor of the Amendment. Subsequently, the measure and a watered-down version failed to get Senate approval.

Perhaps the gravest issue for public policy was the growing concern in America about Communist gains abroad and the dangers of infiltration at home. Americans had been shaken by the loss of China, the Korean War, the rise of Castro and the threat of Communism in the Caribbean, the looming trouble in French Indochina, and the lengthening shadow of the bomb. That month of August, 1953 the Soviets announced the explosion of a hydrogen device. The lawyers felt that membership in the Communist Party was inconsistent with membership in the Bar and was grounds for disqualification for the practice of law. But they also opposed "book burning" and affirmed the "right to read." The vital issue of balancing individual rights with national security, in a Cold War world, would occupy Bill's thoughts as he left Boston and prepared for a year of visiting and speech-making around the land.

The days of the Diamond Jubilee were also a time of transition for Bill and Mildred. They were well acquainted with the Association, but now, in a new way, Bill was feeling the pulse of a major professional body, was sensing the complexities of a national organization that embraced 27 standing committees, 25 special committees, 17 sections with 270 committees engaged in almost all aspects of the legal profession as well as more and more governmental problems. He saw his main task as president to be that of liaison with the various state and local bars, interpreting the A.B.A. to the lawyers of the country. But this particular year there were also on the agenda the completion of the American Bar Center in Chicago and the finishing of an A.B.A. survey of the legal profession financed by a Carnegie Foundation grant. In commenting upon the latter, *The Yellowstone News* observed: "One of the aims of the survey is improvement of the rather deplorable state of the bar's public relations—a job for which Billings' honorable and personable Mr. Jameson is particularly well qualified."[6]

The Missoula folks were with Bill and Mildred in spirit. Early in September Annie reported that she had received a letter from an old Roundup friend, now residing in Yakima, Washington, which read in part:" Was I ever thrilled today as I was looking through the Times Magazine and read about your son ("Willie" as I knew him) as the new president of the A.B.A. Then in glancing through "Life" magazine I saw his picture. He certainly looks natural and I think I would have recognized him if I had met him on the street. He certainly resembles his mother. How proud you must be to have such a fine son! It brought back to mind so many memories of by gone days. I can remember so vividly an Easter program when he recited the 1st Psalm."[7]

It was a deep source of disappointment that Mildred would not be with him during part of the year. Their togetherness had been very much a part of the pattern that had brought him to Boston. But a back problem of long standing had worsened and required spinal fusion. She had first injured her back as a Girl Scout Commissioner collecting grease during wartime to raise money for the program. Now she was scheduled to enter the Mayo Clinic at Rochester, Minnesota for surgery. Fortunately, Mary would be with her. Husband Walker Honaker had received a fellowship in internal medicine at the Clinic. Mary went ahead and found a house to which Mildred could come for convalescence after her month in the hospital. Bill, of course, was in daily contact and stopped off for visits whenever his travels took him nearby. Notes from Association wives assured Mildred that she was being missed at the meetings and that she would be warmly welcomed back. One of her chief disappointments was missing out on a dinner at the White House, when the Eisenhowers invited the Supreme Court Justices, the A.B.A. president and wives for an evening together. But a nice letter from Mamie helped.

III.

So the year began for the A.B.A.'s 77th President. In his first "President's Page" in the *Association Journal,* he expressed his "deep and humble gratitude for the confidence of my fellow lawyers and the high honor they have conferred upon a 'country lawyer.' " During his tenure, there would be brought to completion "two of the most significant projects in the history of the

Association,—the completion of the reports and recommendations of the Survey of the Legal Profession, and the construction of the American Bar Center." The Survey had been in the making since 1947, "as a broad study of the functioning of lawyers in a free society." "The reports of the Survey contain the factual data on our profession,—some encouraging, some disturbing, but all pointing the way to the organized Bar for greater service to the public and the profession."[8]

Equally propitious was the projected completion of the American Bar Center. This splendid facility, costing two million dollars, was scheduled for dedication debt free in August of 1954. It was being financed by a bequest of $400,000, a building fund of $250,000 and $1,500,000 in gifts from lawyers around the country. It would provide headquarters for the A.B.A. and affiliated organizations, a library, a center for research, and a clearing house of research activity in the field of law. It would signal a new era of growth and vastly expanded services for the profession. Meanwhile, Bill would have to operate out of the rented building on North Dearborn Street in Chicago with very limited staffing. Even so, the Association added 5,000 members during his year. One of the reasons was a modified membership policy that was less cumbersome in its procedures and less restrictive in no longer screening candidates on the basis of race, among other considerations.

Less than three weeks after Boston, Bill was giving his first major address at the Annual Conference of the National Institute of Municipal Law Officers at the Mayflower Hotel in Washington. He turned to the topic which would be central in his thoughts during the year, "Balancing Individual Rights with National Security." He was impressed with the wisdom of the founding fathers in "establishing a government which would provide the maximum of individual liberty consistent with a stable, progressive society." That mattered to all who valued individual human personality. "It is the basic distinction between our form of government and the advocates of statism who, like *Hitler*, upheld 'the doctrine of the nothingness and insignificance of the human being,' or *Karl Marx* who argued that the democratic concept that every man is a sovereign being is false, and the 'illusion, dream and postulate of Christianity.' "[9]

The preservation of liberty necessarily meant limitation on the powers of government. Nothing was more basic to the thinking of the founding fathers. The powers of government, Washington had affirmed, are "like fire, a dangerous servant and a fearful master." So, sagaciously, he and the other framers had devised a separation of powers in three branches of government and in other ways provided for "a government of laws and not of men." The tremendous growth during the twentieth century in the size and powers of the executive branch posed a threat to constitutional government. While there are functions proper for Washington that were not envisioned by the framers, there are others " now performed by the federal government which could be exercised as well, or better, by state and local governments." The answer, as Montesquieu had explained, was for the several branches of government to "move in concert" for the general welfare of the people.

The problem of balancing individual rights with national security found particular focus in the Communist threat. Bill noted that at the Boston meeting two A.B.A. committees had dealt with that issue, namely, the Special Committee on Communist Tactics and the Special Committee on Individual Rights. Their two reports, he felt, suggested a "sound balance" between the protection of individual rights and the safeguarding of national security. The first committee, after a three-year study, had issued a Brief finding "that the Communist Party program contemplates the establishment of a dictatorship 'untrammeled by law,' that its all powerful state was dedicated to the destruction by force of all that our constitutional system was designed to protect." The lawyer, by reason of his training, bears a particular responsibility in the struggle for the survival of constitutional government. The role of the Bar in the defense of liberty is both "delicate and vital." So incompatible are the doctrines of Communism with the rule of law that the A.B.A. had moved to expel Association members who belonged to the party or advocated Marxism-Leninism. Lawyers, as citizens, retained all constitutional rights, including the right not to testify if their testimony might tend to incriminate them. In asserting that right, however, the lawyer disclosed disqualification for the practice of law.

The Special Committee on Individual Rights affirmed "the freedom to read" as "a corollary of the Constitutional guarantee of freedom of the press and American lawyers should oppose efforts to restrict it." Similarly, the right of an accused person to the benefit of counsel should not be compromised however unpopular the defendant or his cause might be. Bill recalled for his hearers the case of John Adams who defended the British soldiers involved in the highly emotional Boston Massacre. Interest in procedures be-

Board of Governors, 1953-54 Association Year

ing used in Congressional investigations prompted the House of Delegates to authorize its Special Committee on Individual Rights to study the matter and report to the midwinter meeting in Atlanta.

For the new A.B.A. President, there was no more important problem confronting the American people than "the continued maintenance of a government of law and not of men, with a proper balance between individual rights and national security." In summary, he urged:

> Let us recognize and protect the Constitutional rights of all of our citizens, including Communists, but let us not be blinded to the fact that if the Communist philosophy should prevail, these Constitutional rights would be forever lost.
>
> Let us make certain that all accused, including Communists, have a fair trial or hearing under recognized standards and rules of procedure, but let us not condemn as "witch-hunting" all efforts to rid our government, our profession and our schools of the disciples of Communism or condemn as "stool pigeons" those who espoused Communism in the past and are now willing to testify under oath to expose its aims and purposes.
>
> Let us recognize the rights of all citizens, including Communists, to refuse to testify with respect to alleged Communist activities on the ground of self-incrimination, in the

absence of a statute granting immunity from persecution, but let us also recognize that a reliance upon this right should, in itself, disqualify them from service in our government, our profession and our schools.

Let us be zealous in the protection of individual rights, but, at the same time, be equally zealous in safeguarding our national security.

We have a challenge to leadership in this all important task of maintaining the proper balance between government and men, between individual rights and national security. May we accept this challenge and rededicate ourselves to an intelligent and effective defense of Constitutional liberty.[10]

IV.

In late October Bill was in Denver, enroute to Colorado Springs and speeches before the County Judges Association and the State Bar. At a press conference in the mile-high city, he agreed (not speaking for the A.B.A.) with Attorney-General Herbert Brownell's proposal for a new system of paid public defenders in the federal courts. The existing practice in federal and most state courts relied on appointed (without fee) attorneys to represent persons accused of crimes and who could not afford counsel. That could mean that their cases received inadequate attention and so they were denied fair trials. For Bill, Brownell's proposal was another means of assuring that justice was not contingent upon economic well-being. It had the same general purpose as the legal aid program which he had long supported. From Colorado Springs he dropped down to Albuquerque to meet with the New Mexico Bar, before returning to Chicago for A.B.A. meetings and area speaking engagements.

November 2nd was a red-letter day on his calendar. He joined other Association notables in laying the cornerstone of the American Bar Center on a beautiful campus site donated by the University of Chicago. His predecessor, Robert Storey of Texas, along with others, had worked hard to make the event possible. His good friend, Mr. Justice Jackson, who was so supportive of the A.B.A., spoke at the ceremony and aptly described the future building as a "cathedral to testify to our faith in the rule of law." There was still much to be done, as the Association was resolved to dedicate the Center debt-free the following August. Eventually more than 31,000 gifts and pledges were to be received towards its completion.

At Fayetteville, Arkansas a new law school building was awaiting dedication, and Bill joined Senator William J. Fulbright and other dignitaries for that occasion. Fulbright was a fellow attorney, Rhodes Scholar, and university president, before going to Congress in 1942. The Fulbright Act of 1946 provided for the exchange of teachers and students between the United States and many foreign countries and brought him an international reputation. In his address, Bill returned to the concerns he had shared with the municipal law officers in Washington, namely, the balancing of individual rights with national security.

From Arkansas he traveled to Nebraska, visiting the state bar, and then returned to home base at North Dearborn Street. Thanksgiving Day found him in Rochester, relaxing with Mary and her family, enjoying the grandchildren, relishing the roast turkey and homecooked food, and spending as much time as possible with Mildred in the hospital. Even during this interlude, however, a secretary arrived with matters that needed his immediate attention.

He took a bus from Rochester to the Twin Cities, to present a Bar Association safety award to Governor C. Elmer Anderson for the State of Minnesota. That was the closest he had gotten to Billings since late October. He told reporters from the *Minneapolis Sunday Tribune* that he was spending 75 percent of his time on the road. He noted that at times his schedule bordered on the impossible, as when he was in South Carolina to make a single speech and found himself giving four in the short space of a few hours. In a six minute radio interview, he was asked, just before going on the air, to discuss the Bricker Amendment, the A.B.A. efforts to eliminate legal delays, the relation between the bar and the press, and what the A.B.A. was doing in the field of uniform legislation.[11] Not even Gamaliel, the learned Pharisee of New Testament times, was faced with a more insurmountable task when he was asked to recite the law while standing on one foot!

A particularly happy occasion came on December 19th, when he returned to Montana and to Missoula for the School of Law's Anniversary Law Dinner at the Hotel Florence. Over 400 people had come in from all over the state. He was one of four men being honored that evening for their accomplishments in the field of law. Others were former Dean A.N. Whitlock, now of Lexington, Kentucky, Russell D. Niles, Dean of the N.Y. University School of

Law and a Missoula graduate, and Dean C.W. Leaphart who would be retiring in the spring after nearly forty years of service to the Law School.

Bill was introduced by Judge Walter L. Pope, former faculty member at Missoula and then on the Ninth Circuit of Appeals in San Francisco, who traced his friend's rise in th A.B.A. since 1936. In his remarks, Bill reviewed his work with this home state audience and described, in particular, the Association's survey of the legal profession and the forthcoming completion of the Bar Center. He noted that Montana lawyers had contributed more than $9000 to the cause.

The principal speaker of the evening was Judge Harold R. Medina of the U.S. Court of Appeals for the Second Circuit. The nationally prominent jurist was "glad to be here and help you whoop it up for Bill. He'll do a grand job as president of the American Bar Association and it's fine to help him celebrate." Medina had been appointed by President Truman in 1947 as judge on the U.S. District Court, Southern District of New York, and it was in that capacity that he had gained national attention in presiding over the nine-month trial (January to October, 1949) of 11 Communists charged with conspiracy to teach and advocate the violent overthrow of the U.S. Government. It was an experience in tension, abuse, and high emotion that he would always remember. The conviction of the Communists and Medina's handling of the trial were upheld by the U.S. Supreme Court. So he had had his moments on the bench when he spoke to the Missoula gathering on "The Education of a Judge—Chapter II." Later, Bill and Medina would serve together on the Second Circuit Court and particularly enjoy their associations.

In January, as something different in his routine, he received a phone call from Secretary of Defense Charles Wilson who wanted to talk with him in Washington. Bill noted that he was due there the following week and would come by. Wilson liked what he had been hearing about the new A.B.A. president and wanted him as chief counsel for the Defense Department. Bill was naturally pleased but couldn't consider it, as he had seven months to go with the A.B.A. More than that, deep down, he was not really interested in moving away from his Montana home base. Years after, he would have no regrets about such career opportunities turned aside.

Later that month, he was on the West Coast, speaking to the Los Angeles Bar Association and reiterating his position with regard to

Bill photographed with stars Barbara Rush, Janet Leigh and Tony Curtis while touring Universal Studios in Hollywood.

Fifth Amendment uses. Any American citizen, he declared at a luncheon meeting at the Biltmore Bowl, has a perfect right to avoid self-incrimnation by appealing to the Fifth Amendment, but in so doing he or she should become disqualified from holding any governmental office of trust, including teaching in the schools, and from the practice of law. He hoped that Congress would provide the necessary legislation for an immunity statute with proper safeguards so that the government could compel the giving of testimony vital to national defense. "As American citizens," he concluded, "all of us have an obligation to assume leadership in upholding our Constitution and form of government, and in exposing the dangers of Communism and its activities. There is a crying need for a fair and intelligent presentation of both the principles and facts. The defense of our Constitutional rights and freedoms should not depend upon our economic, social or political viewpoints, but should apply equally to all persons and be administered fairly under all circumstances."[12]

The California stay included luncheon at Universal Motion Picture Studios, where he posed with popular "stars" of the time, and visits with the Sacramento Bar and at the Berkeley and Stanford Law Schools. Then the seemingly tireless president trained back East for a day or two at A.B.A. headquarters and then another speech before the St. Louis Bar. His repeated theme of the protection of individual rights and of the public welfare was picked up in an editorial in the Patterson, New Jersey *Evening News*. "If more

Congressmen, and more citizens, could achieve the same balanced judgement exhibited by President William J. Jameson of the American Bar Association, there would be a great deal less smear forays in Washington, less fear over security, less hysteria and tension generally. . . . The pervading sentiment and decision of a people should be dictated by a balanced perspective, to which Mr. Jameson gave articulate guidance."[13]

The first of March brought the Midyear Meeting of the House of Delegates and a regional meeting of the A.B.A. in Atlanta and a particularly busy but happy time. Mildred was able to be with him once more. Their travels that month included several stops in the East before heading West for two memorable occasions in Billings and Butte. Saturday evening, March 21, there was a William J. "Bill" Jameson Appreciation Dinner at the Shrine Auditorium, sponsored jointly by the Yellowstone Bar and the Chamber of Commerce, with hundreds of his fellow citizens in attendance. It was there that Attorney Horace Davis quipped that " 'Bill' Jameson is only 99.44 percent pure. I happen to know that he voted Democratic in 1920." It felt good to be home, as he outlined for the familiar audience the program and main activities of the A.B.A. Two days later he was at the Finlen Hotel in Butte, noting that he had traveled 38,000 miles in the past few months but that "I can't think of any occasion which has given me more pleasure than this chance to address the Butte Exchange Club in my home town—my native home town." The kid from McKinley grade school had indeed gone a long way!

V.

Aside from the pleasantness of the occasion, Bill had another reason to remember the testimonial dinner in Billings. That was the day he received a phone call which would involve him in the McCarthy controversy. It had begun back in February, 1950 at Wheeling, West Virginia when the little-known junior senator from Wisconsin chose a Lincoln's Day speech to claim that he knew of 205 card-carrying Communists in the State Department. From that time, the unsubstantiated charges multiplied, made plausible, in some measure, by the uneasiness of many Americans about the Communist threat. His tactics became labeled as McCarthyism and had a significance in the life of the country beyond the influence of the man. It was a way of thinking and acting that ignored personal liberties and constitutional processes, which had preceded him and would outlast his reign of power in Washington. The real crescendo of McCarthyism happened to coincide with Bill's presidency and involved the senator's quest for Communists in the U.S. Army.

By March of 1954 McCarthy's Senate Investigating Subcommittee was locked in an exchange of conflicting charges with Secretary of the Army Stevens and his aides. Committee member Stuart Symington of Missouri was concerned that the Senate was getting a bad name with McCarthy acting as "accusing witness, prosecutor and judge." He felt that the controversial chairman should remove himself from the Army investigation. The suggestion had been rejected previously by McCarthy, who was away on a speaking tour and had left Senator Karl Mundt of South Dakota in charge. It was Mundt and Senator McClelland of Arkansas who placed the call to Billings, inquiring if the A.B.A. president was willing to serve as special counsel for the subcommittee. They thought that it would take not more than three weeks to clarify matters with the Army and, on that basis, Bill's first inclination was to accept the assignment. However, he informed Mundt that it would be necessary to confer with the Association's Board of Governors.

Meanwhile, the press was paying close attention. *The Billings Gazette* for March 21 reported Symington's unhappiness and that Senator Mundt was involved "in a mysterious quest for a special counsel to direct the subcommittee's projected probe of its own chairman and his difference with officials of the Army dept." Further, he and Senator McClelland of Arkansas, the senior Democrat on the Committee, had settled on a "nationally prominent attorney" who, by report (it was erroneous) didn't want to be bothered but, upon further urging, promised to think it over. Mundt was quoted as adding: "We said we would give him the right to pick his own staff, fix the ground rules and stage what we hope will be a model for congressional investigating procedure. The public will accept him if he agrees, as a man of outstanding ability and complete impartiality."

By the 23rd the *Great Falls Tribune* was reporting that Mundt had identified the mystery attorney and he was none other than A.B.A. President Bill Jameson of Billings. He had declined the assignment as inappropriate for him in view of his heavy commitments to the Association. Two days later, the *Yellowstone*

News observed that Jameson had "ruefully passed up the chance to write a page of American history. Saturday night, as the community poured out its praise at a gracious, garrulous testimonial banquet for the first Montanan to lead the American Bar, the guest of honor wrestled with one of the most difficult decisions of his career."

In his "President's Page" for May in the *A.B.A. Journal,* Bill reviewed actions taken and the reasons for not accepting the assignment. Following the phone call, he had conferred with the Board of Governors and the chairmen of the Committees on Individual Rights and National Security and Communist Tactics. This group voted 11 to 4 against his taking the responsibility. Former Senator O'Connor of Maryland was chairing the Committee on Communist Tactics and wired that in his opinion the job of special counsel would last most of the summer and would do the Association no good. His prediction as to time proved to be accurate. It was not an easy decision, in view of the A.B.A.'s desire to cooperate with Congress and to render public service. But the majority opinion, in which he concurred, was that acceptance was inadvisable because of his existing commitments leading up to the Annual Meeting and, also, by reason of possible political implications in the controversy.

Communications from Association members reflected an overwhelming support of their leaders' decision, though, inevitably, the nature of the controversy made for a sharp polarization of views. One wire read: "Legal cowards die many times before their death; the valiant like McCarthy never taste of death but once," and another: "What fools ye mortals be who won't stand up for the *one* man who is trying to save our country." Equally vehement was the regret that the A.B.A. leadership had "ducked the opportunity of investigating and maybe exposing *the* evil of our day—McCarthyism," and another letter urging "the Association to do everything possible to achieve the expulsion of McCarthy from our United States Senate."[14]

The three-week investigation which Senator Mundt had projected turned into a television spectacular that lasted from April 22 to June 17. And it proved to be the beginning of the end for Senator Joseph McCarthy. He blundered badly in assailing the army in a Cold War world and in impugning the motives of high public officials, not excepting the occupant of the White House. Television brought the man and his methods into the living rooms of millions of Americans, his bullying tactics, rude intrusions, and irrelevant comments and insinuations. Even his supporters did not like what they saw. Then came the climactic moment when the army's mild-mannered counsel, Attorney Joseph Welsh of Boston, roused by needless accusations against a young associate, exploded: "Until this moment, Senator, I think I never really gauged your cruelty or your recklessness. . . . If it were in my power to forgive you for your reckless cruelty, I would do so. I like to think I am a gentle man, but your forgiveness will have to come from someone other than me. . . . Have you no sense of decency, sir, at long last?"[15]

So long accustomed to power and its abuses, McCarthy was uncomprehending as his star went into rapid eclipse. In December of 1954 the Senate voted overwhelmingly (67 to 22) to "condemn" him for conduct unbecoming a member of that body. His backing virtually vanished by the time of his death three years later. Meanwhile, about the time the hearings were closing, Bill was in Spokane addressing the local bar association. A very attractive woman reporter came to interview him, with a photographer. She began by asking, "Aren't you glad you didn't take on that McCarthy investigation?" He replied that he had been limiting his comments to the reasons for not doing so. She then arranged for the photographer to take his picture, saying, "Now, let's have a big smile." He couldn't very well refuse. The next day his picture was on the front page of the *Spokesman Review*, with the headline: "Bar President happy he didn't take on McCarthy investigation." In fact, as he had watched the parade of personalities in the televised drama, he was reassured in the wisdom of his decision and that of the Board of Governors not to have become involved.

VI.

While the Army-McCarthy hearings were going on, the Supreme Court on May 17 made the headlines with a historic ruling on school desegregation. *Brown v. Board of Education of Topeka, Kansas* reversed the position of an earlier court in *Plessy v. Ferguson* of 1896. Chief Justice Earl Warren and his Associate Justices delivered a unanimous opinion that found segregated schools to be unconstitutional, depriving children on the basis of race "of the equal protection of the laws guaranteed by the Fourteenth Amendment." Bill was visiting with the Mississippi Bar at the time the Court's decision was made public. A group of lawyers invited him to breakfast and asked if he could not work to have the A.B.A. file a petition to get the Court to reconsider. Fortunately, a member of the Board of Governors was from Mississippi and proceeded to have the petition quashed. Rather than support such a move, Bill was providing leadership to modify the A.B.A. membership policy so that Blacks would no longer be excluded.

Earlier that month he had been in Missoula visiting the Law School. At a luncheon in his honor at the Hotel Florence, he shared some of his insights about the profession with local attorneys, faculty, and students. "The most common complaint today against young lawyers," he found, "is their use of the English language. It apparently is the hardest of the languages for law students to master." It is important to continue one's studies and to read great works of American and English literature. "A knowledge of great literature can make the difference between a great lawyer and a mere attorney." Bill also urged that young lawyers cultivate humility in their relations with clients and the public. Further, the new attorney should not be tempted to "pull his rank" with legal secretaries. Very importantly, brilliance is no substitute for thorough preparation of cases. "The old adage that the law is a jealous mistress is still true today. Lawyers don't get by on an eight-hour day or a 40-hour week." The A.B.A. President had also found a good sense of humor to be "necessary equipment for this job."[16]

May took him to Portland, Oregon, as well, for the second regional A.B.A. meeting of the year. More than 1000 lawyers were present from the eight-state area of California, Nevada, Oregon, Washington, Idaho, Montana, Wyoming, and Utah. The agenda ranged over such topics as congressional investigations, Latin America and world affairs, effects of the atom bomb and the supersonic age on the Pacific Northwest, and proposals to tighten regulations on newspaper and radio coverage of court trials.[17] Mildred and Mrs. Loyd Wright of Los Angeles, whose husband was succeeding Bill as A.B.A. president, were quoted in the local press as being very agreeable to "conventioning" and glad that their husbands didn't want to "stag it" like some men. Mrs. Wright noted Mildred's absence from earlier meetings and declared that she was the "most missed person" she had ever known at A.B.A. functions.

By the first of June, Bill figured that he had traveled a distance equal to three times around the world!On the 4th he was introduced at the Iowa State Bar Association as the A.B.A. President who had traveled 75,000 miles on 15 gallons of ginger ale! Fortunately for the Association's budget, he had a railway pass (as division counsel for the Northern Pacific) and saved considerable money traveling by train. That also was a good way to get work done while going from place to place. There were times, however, when scheduling was so jammed that only the plane could get him around. That was the case in June as he criss-crossed the country, touching places as far removed as Maine and Minnesota. By the end of his term, he would have visited state and local bar associations and law schools in 38 states! While much of his time was taken with such visitation, there were also the demanding administrative duties which took him frequently to North Dearborn Street in Chicago. There was no vice president or executive director for backup assistance and the Association staff was very limited.

More and more, as spring eased into summer, Bill's thoughts were turning to the Annual Meeting in August, but first there was the yearly gathering of his own State Bar in Billings in late July. He could compliment Montana on being the first state to raise its quota of funds for the American Bar Center. In fact, Montana lawyers had exceeded their quota by 143%, an oversubscription surpassed only by New York State! Then in the restfulness of Camp Senia, he pondered the year that was ending and worked on his address for the Annual Meeting. So much had transpired in a crowded twelve months. How could its meaning best be distilled in a presentation of thirty minutes?

What he found to be "an exceedingly interesting and pleasant year" climaxed at the 77th Annual Meeting of the A.B.A. at the Conrad Hilton in Chicago. Such was the magnitude of activities planned that Chief Justice Walter V. Shaefer of the Illinois Supreme Court welcomed the 5000 delegates to a "three ring circus." Sunday evening, August 15, members and wives gathered for an open air concert in Grant Park, where they enjoyed breezes off Lake Michigan as they listened to the strains of Puccini's *Madame Butterfly*. Bill was particularly pleased that this time his mother and sister along with Mary, Walker and the children could be with him and Mildred. In a sense, it had all begun with a father and a mother nurturing the dreams and ambitions of a small boy in a little Montana mining town.

The opening session on Monday featured the President's Annual Address and Bill had carefully selected a topic which focused, he felt, on the mission of the A.B.A.: "Service to the Public and the Profession—a Reappraisal." The past year had been an eventful one and emphasized the need to evaluate and reappraise Association policies and programs. He recalled the issues that had been high on the year's agenda: the Bricker Amendment, the ongoing debate over A.B.A. involvement in public concerns, the question of the inclusion of lawyers in Social Security, the reports and recommendations of the Committees on Communist Tactics and Individual Rights as Affected by National Security, and the discussion over the President's role in the Army-McCarthy controversy.

Implicit in the actions that had been taken was the role of a House of Delegates now with 222 members and representative of the great body of American attorneys. Implied, also, was the new direction which the Association had been taking in recent years of participation in public problems, in line with the constitutional amendment of 1949 and the adopted recommendations of the Committee on Scope and Correlation of Work. Implied, too, was a basic commitment to a "balance perspective" in seeking to preserve the rights of the individual in a free society facing the threat of international communism.

As the 77th President surveyed his year in office, he felt that the Association could take "particular satisfaction" in the completion and financing of the American Bar Center and the "establishment of the research center as a going concern, with substantial progress in the first major research project of preparing a design for a comprehensive study of the administration of criminal justice." In addition, there had been formulation "of plans for utilizing and implementing the reports and recommendations of the Survey of the Legal Profession in an expanded program of service to the public and the profession." The year had witnessed a record increase in membership, gains in making the A.B.A. more representative of the whole legal community, a more "enlightened program of public relations," increased emphasis on continuing legal education for the practicing attorney, and ongoing progress with regard to the Association's long-range public objectives.

In summarizing the Association's obligations and opportunities, he quoted the late William L. Ransom:

> The times impose on the organized bar new duties and new opportunities for leadership of informed public opinion. We are not living or carrying on our work in the era or mood of 1878. We can not put in our own way the barriers and hurdles of narrow and ancient concepts of our objectives.

Participants in Dedication of American Bar Center, 1954

> Whatever goes to the heart of defending and maintaining our Constitution, our laws, our form of government, and the right of men to live their lives in freedom from other's tyranny must be within our Association's province unless we are to fail our country and ourselves.[18]

That part of the week that did not make the headlines involved the numerous meetings of committees and sections. "From their patient, laborious, careful, often painstaking routine come the resolutions and recommendations that the House of Delegates is requested to act upon."[19] The House itself held six sessions, "which were marked with oratory, hard work, serious debate, occasional sharp disagreement and biting humor." After lengthy discussion, the House adopted a uniform code for the conduct of congressional investigations to be submitted to Congress, but tabled a proposal to teach Communism in the schools as a means of pointing up "the superiority of democratic over collectivist government." The issue of inclusion of lawyers in the Social Security Program, which had been before the Association for several years, was again referred for further study.

Two issues of growing importance for the A.B.A. were raised by speakers from the high court. At a luncheon on Tuesday, Chief

Opening the new A.B.A. Center

Justice Earl Warren stressed the need for legal aid for the poor. "There are millions of people in this country," he declared, "who live on the ragged edge of nothing and who do not have available to them the services of any lawyer. They are fearful of lawyers and fearful of courts because of the costs involved."[20] Such people need to know that lawyers have a heart and are concerned to see that their individual rights are preserved. Bill also addressed the luncheon, noting that progress had been made but that a continuing emphasis on legal aid work was essential.

Associate Justice Robert H. Jackson, who had served on the Nuremberg Tribunal for Nazi war criminals, strongly criticized the administration of criminal law in a report to the House of Delegates. Jackson was chairing an Association special committee charged with a survey of criminal justice. "The need for overhauling our criminal procedures," he pointed out, "is apparent in each day's news." He noted the "high level dissatisfaction with the conflicting, confused, and antiquated procedures which now prevail in our country to the delight of the guilty, and the prejudice, in many instances, of the really innocent."[21] He was identifying a problem area in which his good friend, Bill Jameson, would take a deep interest after his appointment to the federal bench.

The weather that week was typically Chicago— "changeable, unpredictable, capricious, sometimes violent," as one source

Mother and Lucille, 1955

described it.[22] But Thursday was warm and sunny for the dedication of the new American Bar Center. In ceremonies at Rockefeller Chapel, Chief Justice Warren dedicated the handsome new facility to "improvement of the administration of justice." "We believe," he said, "that so long as human nature is such as it is, there must be a constant struggle to preserve our freedoms. We do not propose to let nature take its course. On the contrary, we are determined here to create the climate essential to the constant improvement of both the text of our law and its application to the affairs of people. . . . As lawyers, we know better than most that there are defects in our administration of justice. With adequate research we can strengthen our leadership in remedying them."[23] The A.B.A. President read a letter of congratulations from the White House and then led the procession from the grey, gothic chapel across the Midway to the white, modern structure of simple lines. There the newly designed flag of the Association was raised, along with Old Glory, and he cut the ceremonial ribbon at the main entrance.

The threshold they crossed that day also symbolized entering a new era, when membership was expected to soar and the Association would render vastly improved services to the profession and to the public at large. Chicago, then, was a new beginning—and for Bill as well. He had reached an important milestone in his journey with the A.B.A., but there were other assignments worth doing and, as the poet said, other promises to keep. Chicago was also a moment that fulfilled Annie's fondest dreams. At the final dinner, when the President of the Canadian Bar spoke, he observed that the A.B.A. was fortunate to have a president so young that his mother could be present. He asked her to rise—and the girl from Butte, the wife of the Roundup lawyer—received a standing ovation. She looked, Lucille later remembered, so shy and so sweet.

CHAPTER SEVEN

JUDGE JAMESON

Once, years later, Bill was preparing to spend a birthday at Camp Senia and his law clerk was assisting in carrying briefcase after briefcase to the car. When the young man wondered aloud why the Judge was taking so much of the office to the mountains, Bill smiled and explained, "Martin, I enjoy my work; I love the law."[1]

That kind of enthusiasm for the daily task was now focused on an accumulation of affairs at Coleman, Jameson and Lamey. The firm he had joined back in 1922 had become one of the largest and busiest in the state, employing more than a dozen attorneys. His role in the organization was such that when he resigned to go on the federal bench, it took more than one new lawyer to replace him. The firm continued as counsel for the Northern Pacific; and Bill remained as chairman of the Montana Railroad Association. So there was no downshifting as the A.B.A. Past President returned home.

On the larger scene, he would remain a member of the House of Delegates and attend its meetings twice yearly. That perpetuated what he valued most—the friendships he had made in the Association across the years. There would be other important posts in the legal world and other assignments for the public servant. Meanwhile, in September, 1954 he traveled to Winnipeg to attend the

Conferring Honorary Degree, University of Manitoba, 1954

36th Annual Meeting of the Canadian Bar Association and to receive an honorary degree from the University of Manitoba. In October, Vice President Richard Nixon was in Billings, on a campaign trail for Republican candidates in the upcoming Congressional elections. He noted that Montana had produced "many fine men" for the nation, and prominent among them was William J. Jameson, who had served the A.B.A. with distinction, making "a fine impression all over America. Montana should be proud of him."[2] It was the Vice President who suggested Bill as Special Counsel for the Senate Investigating Subcommittee.

A particularly interesting assignment came along in November. President Eisenhower named him to a Commission, authorized by Congress in July, to study the application of federal laws to the Virgin Islands. He was one of seven members, and in the organization meeting in Washington he was designated chairman. Congress directed that the Commission should submit its recommendations by the following July, so Bill and his colleagues geared up with a consultant from the Boston University Law School and with a staff headquartered at the Harvard Law School in Cambridge. The Commission proceeded to solicit information and advice from all members of the Cabinet, numerous affected agencies and commissions of the United States, and the Governor and other individuals and organizations of the Virgin Islands.

In March the Commission held public hearings on St. Thomas and St. Croix. At meetings in Washington in late May and Cambridge in late June, the final recommendations were readied for Congress with respect to statutes then inapplicable which should be made applicable, statutes of doubtful applicability which should be made expressly applicable, and statutes then applicable which should be amended or made inapplicable. One particular statute was settled for the Commission by the Supreme Court in holding that the new easy divorce law of the Virgin Islands was unconstitutional.

One of the major problems the Commission encountered involved the immigration laws and, especially, the practice of aliens to remain beyond the time permitted. Many residents of the British Virgin Islands came to the American Islands to work on farms, in hotels, and to do other forms of manual labor. This kind of employment was often available as many natives of the American Islands left home for the so-called "pen jobs" or office work in the United States. Immigration concerns took the Commission to the British Island of Tortola, where they were met by the thirteen members of the legislature, spent some time in a discussion of mutual concerns, and then were entertained by the Governor and his wife. Bill and his friends were impressed with the Governor's English lady and were surprised to learn later that she had grown up in Brooklyn! Three members of the Commission were from the Virgin islands, two of whom were black, and that posed problems finding hotel accommodations in Washington in the days before the Civil Rights Movement. All in all, it was the kind of assignment that he enjoyed and that made for good telling to his acquaintances back in Billings.

Shortly after leaving the A.B.A. presidency, Bill was given one of his more complicated and delicate tasks in chairing the Association's Special Committee on Professional Relations. At hand was a two-year effort to resolve differences between lawyers and accountants, especially with regard to their Treasury practice. Dean

Erwin N. Griswold of the Harvard Law School felt that his Montana friend was a particularly happy choice. Surveying the Committee's progress in the *A.B.A. Journal* for December, 1955, he did not see how the Association could have a better representative. "William J. Jameson has been patient, fair, reasonable, pleasant, earnest, genial, firm, always willing to hear all sides, open-minded, in short everything that the chairman of such a committee should be."

Bill did succeed in developing a consensus between his committee and the parallel committee of the American Institute of Accountants to formulate procedures for resolving differences "by conference and cooperation." In the course of this assisngment, he spoke to the Montana Society of Certified Public Accountants in Butte and to the American Institute of Accountants at the annual meeting in Seattle. The final report, in December of 1956, recommended "that there be established, in every state, a joint conference committee of lawyers and certified public accountants to consider disputes as they may arise and to attempt to settle them by negotiation. Special committees of the A.B.A. and the A.I.A. would function similarly on the national level as the 'National Conference' and endeavor to assist state committees in resolving local differences."[3]

Less fraught with controversy was his election as President of the American Judicature Society at its annual meeting in Dallas in August of 1956. That capped a long record of activity and leadership in the Society, which existed to promote the effective administration of justice. To that end, the Society published its *Journal* and other literature, sponsored conferences and seminars, maintained an information and consultation service, supported research, and operated The Center for Judicial Conduct Organizations. The Society was headquartered at the new Bar Center, with membership open to all persons interested in court improvement.

II.

These and other involvements with the organized Bar, together with the busy schedule at the office, filled his days and left little time or inclination to ponder further career developments. Yet, there was an underlying interest in the court system, an appreciation for the dignity and integrity of the judgeship, that was stirred with Charles N. Pray's announcement in January, 1957 of his

Swearing In Ceremony, 1957

retirement from the bench. The venerable jurist had reached 88 and had a record 33 years as a federal judge. He was the oldest judge in point of service in the 9th Judicial District.

Bill's friends had been urging his consideration for the federal bench and one, in particular, communicated with the White House. Governor J. Hugo Aronson wrote to President Eisenhower that Bill was "a personal friend of mine," and "one of Montana's most distinguished sons." "He is 100 per cent honest, straightforward, unimpeachable, and of the very highest character." His record, including his A.B.A. presidency, was clear evidence that he was "one of Montana's outstanding attorneys."[4] Other testimonials were equally enthusiastic and on March 5th the President nominated Bill to be a U.S. district judge for Montana. He was in Helena, at the Montana Railroad Association office, when he first got the news. "Naturally, I am pleased at the appointment," he told the press, and then added: "Judge Pray has been one of the most distinguished and best loved of our federal judges."[5]

The Yellowstone News for March 7th headlined the nomination story with "Billings Gains Its First Federal Judicial Post." Bill had brought a second major distinction to his adopted town. Actually, it was a sobering time, along with all of the congratulations, for going to the federal bench meant a break with much that had given him genuine satisfaction. His active role in Republican politics would now be left behind, with only the memories of grooming candidates, raising money, and hitting the campaign trail with a pocketfull of speeches.

Similarly, he would have to forego serving on community boards and committees where solicitation of funds was involved and so resigned from the boards of the Deaconess Hospital and the Y.M.C.A. But what mattered most was closing out his career as a trial lawyer, which was the aspect of the law that had first engaged his youthful attention. It was obvious that he was in his element in the courtroom and had found fulfillment practicing before the bar. Yet, those same qualities of intellectual vigor, integrity, fairness, and deep humanity were needed on the bench and there, too, he would soon feel at home.

Somewhere in Washington communications misfired and Bill was not informed when his Senate hearing was to occur. On the day scheduled, he was enjoying a bath in his Billings home when the phone rang. Mildred answered, and it was someone from the Attorney General's Office wanting to know where he was! With his kind of endorsements, however, the Senate confirmation was voted on March 27, without his appearance, and on April 11 he was officially sworn in.

The Billings Gazette for April 12 reported that the courtroom in the Federal Building was filled and a crowd in excess of 250 overflowed into the halls. Federal Judge William D. Murray of Butte administered the oath to the ninth federal district judge in the history of the state. "In the history of Montana," he commented, "and of all the West, and perhaps even in all the United States, there has been no man assume the federal bench, who by his record and in the esteem of all who know him, was more qualified to assume the deep responsibilities of the judiciary." Bill was presented to the court by his longtime partner, Henry J. Coleman, while representatives from the A.B.A., Montana Bar, and Yellowstone County Bar looked on. *The Daily Missoulian* expressed the prevailing sentiment: "In deciding upon William J. Jameson for a Montana district judgeship, President Eisenhower selected one of the Treasure State's best known and most able attorneys to round out his career in a lifetime appointment to the federal bench."[6]

While Bill was being made a federal district judge, he was also selected by the A.B.A., along with James T. Finlen of Butte, western general counsel for the Anaconda Company, and active in the Association, as a Fellow of the newly organized American Bar Foundation. It was a recognition of those "whose professional, public and private careers have demonstrated their outstanding dedication to the welfare of their community and the maintenance of the major objectives of the American Bar Association."[7] The A.B.A.'s president-elect, Charles S. Rhyne, of Washington, D.C., had a further word of commendation for his friend, the new federal judge, in speaking to the Montana Bar Association at Yellowstone Park in June. "Not the least of your contributions to the legal profession was to provide a man of the caliber of Bill Jameson to be president of the American Bar Association. His administration has set a high example for those of us who came after him. And no better qualified lawyer ever became a federal judge."[8]

Meanwhile, the new judge was in Great Falls the middle of May to sit for his first cases there, with his predecessor in attendance. In informal remarks preceding litigation, he expressed the hope that his tenure on the bench would be marked by the same "moral and intellectual honesty" as Judge Pray's. In return, the retired jurist emphasized his delight at being succeeded by a man of Jameson's caliber and predicted an outstanding career on the bench for him. In remarks to the attending counsel, Judge Jameson indicated that he would be automatically disqualifying himself in any litigation wherein his former Billings law firm played a role while he was with the firm. He also urged counsel to bring to his attention any such potential conflicts which he might have overlooked.[9]

III

The appointment to the federal bench ranked with his A.B.A. presidency as twin peaks in his career, but that summer of 1957 held another memorable occasion for Bill and Mildred, one which had been a long time in the making. Back in 1924 the A.B.A. and the Bar Council of England and Wales (the barristers or trial lawyers) had held a very successful joint meeting in London. It had become sort of legendary, so that year after year there had been talk of another pilgrimage to England. At length their long-awaited meeting was planned for July 22 to 29, only the 1957 gathering included the more recently organized Law Society of England (the solicitors or office lawyers) as well. It was, therefore, a much larger assembly than the one in 1924.

Three thousand lawyers and wives embarked on the pilgrimage, intent upon Americanizing London during their stay. Bill and Mildred sailed on the *R.M.S. Queen Mary* and had, she wrote to

Bill and Mildred photographed on board R.M.S "Queen Mary"

the folks in Missoula, "a delightful crossing." She did not need any of the Dramamine. She was excited about meeting the Queen at a royal garden party and thought she had better start practicing her curtsy! The opening ceremonies at Westminster Hall produced some of the best pageantry since the coronation. The ancient structure had been built at the end of the eleventh century and had been long revered as "the very workshop of our law." Everywhere Americans were reminded of the long evolution of the common law, in which their own legal system was grounded.

July 26 brought an occasion of particular interest to Bill and Mildred. He was scheduled to make a response for the A.B.A. at a dinner in the beautiful hall of the Middle Temple. That was one of the four Inns of Court or legal societies whose members have the exclusive right to practice before the bar. Dating from before the 14th century, they took their names from the buildings where schools of law were once held. Bill remembered what Lord Justice Morris, a member of the Middle Temple, had said in addressing the American Bar Association in San Francisco in 1952:

> In your land and mine we have no fear nor shame when we say, 'come and breathe our air and walk among us, and learn our thoughts, and hear our story, and know our hopes, and

> feel the pulse of our way of life.' Happy will be the day when in all the world men and peoples may move freely and without fear, and will come to know each other's minds. But until that day dawns, as well as when it dawns, great causes will be served and preserved if there be no blurring of the concord and amity which binds the peoples who speak the English tongue.[10]

Americans, Bill declared, "like to feel that we are common inheritors with you of the great traditions of the common law, the eternal principle of liberty under law, and the ceaseless pursuit of justice—all nurtured in the Middle Temple and the other Inns of Court." He and his fellow lawyers were indeed glad for "this opportunity to share briefly with you these hallowed landmarks of the law." Reflecting the concerns for world peace that backgrounded the meeting, Bill noted that the A.B.A. had adopted an emphasis on international law as one of its six long-range objectives. "You have been building and rebuilding for centuries. For a brief period we have been building on your basic structure. In the future working together through a friendship rooted in mutual trust and respect...we can contribute to the attainment of the goal of permanent world peace in helping build a government of law throughout the world."

As one of the "hallowed landmarks of the law," the American lawyers gathered in a quiet, green stretch beside the Thames to dedicate a memorial to the Magna Carta. Their dollars had built a small circular temple at Runnymede Meadow, where 742 years earlier King John had consented to limitations on his royal power. "The dedication ceremonies at Runnymede," an American observer later recalled, "were a great spectacle. About 6,000 people made the pilgrimage. Cars were parked all over the meadow; seating arrangements were provided for about 3,000 ticket holders, the rest of the audience standing. President-elect Charles Rhyne of Washington, D.C. and former President E. Smythe Gambrell, of the American Bar Association, delivered the addresses of dedication. Lord Evershed, Master of the Rolls, and Sir Hartley-Shawcross, President of the General Council of the Bar, replied for the English Bar."[11]

On the 29th the Queen entertained the American attorneys and their wives at a Buckingham Palace garden party. The afternoon sky was friendly, with an occasional splash of sunlight, as many Americans moved around somewhat stiffly in gray toppers and morning coats and their wives wore gowns of varied pastel hues, hopefully in keeping with the event. The Queen sought to put them at their ease with miniature hot dogs and hamburgers, introduced at a Buckingham Palace function for the first time. The Queen Mother, who was an honorary "bencher" of the Middle Temple, made the biggest hit with Bill. A quarter of a century later, he would be remembering as one of the high points of his stay in London his chat with this "very delightful" person.

Another world-famous Britisher, Sir Winston Churchill, now 83, chose the lawyers' gathering as the time to come out of virtual seclusion and share with them his concerns about the future of the United Nations. "Justice cannot be a hit-or-miss system. We cannot be content with an arrangement where our system of international laws applies only to those who are willing to keep them."[12] It was a truly memorable time in London. "I am sure," a former A.B.A. president would write, "that every one of us came away feeling that the whole London experience was historic, worthwhile and unforgettable—and that Churchill was quite right in pointing out that if America and England 'work together, there is no doubt that we shall together represent a factor in the development of the whole world which no one will have cause to regret.' "[13]

From London Bill and Mildred visited the Shakespeare country and saw a play at Stratford-on-Avon. Then came a tour of Holland, which Mildred found to be particularly appealing and marveled how much they had done to rebuild after the war. They moved on to Belgium in time for the famous festival in Bruges, with a cast of thousands, staged every five years to commemorate the Crusades. Their thoroughly enjoyable time on the Continent ended in Paris, where they enplaned for the 16-hour flight back to Billings. The British, Mildred reflected later, really outdid themselves to be hospitable. The London pilgrimage had been "a wonderful event—worth millions in friendship, good will, and understanding between two countries."[14]

IV.

Of the various qualities that would shape the Jameson judgeship, none was more fundamental than the compassion he had learned from his mother. Law clerks and others would speak of his uncommon humanity in dealing with those who appeared in his court, regardless of their station in life. He would worry about what was best for an Indian youth caught in a burglary at Wolf Point, while also wrestling with such major matters as the reapportionment of the Montana Legislature. At heart, the law he loved was not punitive only, but, more importantly, possessed the possibilities of being redemptive. And that guided him always in his decisions.

His touch of compassion or humanity from the bench made an important difference in many lives, even that of the hardened con artist who believed that he was beyond changing his ways. One man wrote from California, perhaps expressing the difference best:

> Dear Judge Jameson:
>
> I don't know if you are accustomed to having men you have sent to prison write back to you and thank you or not, but that is the purpose of my letter.
>
> I was sentenced in your court on the 23rd of December, 1959.
>
> I want you to know that your interest and efforts to help me as a person within the framework of the law were not wasted. I was a very bitter and difficult individual but as a result of the efforts of yourself and . . . the attorney you appointed for me, I am now back home, happy and I hope mentally healthy, back in school, and looking forward to a happy and meaningful life. If you had not sentenced me as you did none of this would be true today. A prison sentence alone would have been meaningless. The fact that you ordered psychiatric care and studies made the difference, and the fact that you were concerned played no small role during the months and years in prison.
>
> I have no doubt that if we had more men like you on the benches of our state and federal courts, prisons and all that they stand for would one day be a thing of the past.
>
> With every good wish for a merry Christmas, and many happy new years, I remain

The capacity to care would also be evident in a relationship that so easily could have been one of condescension. Rather, there would be an unforgettable learning experience for the more than thirty law clerks who would serve him during his years as an active and senior judge. "We did not know very much law," one of them would later recall, "and we did not know very much about lawyering, but we were always treated with the utmost in professional respect. Actually it was more than that. We were treated as professional equals."[15]

And from another: "In a very real sense he made one feel like an equal. . .asking my advice on various legal issues, sharing thoughts with me on different cases on which he was working. He never failed to stop by my office each night before he left this building to wish me a good evening."[16]

But there was nothing soft or sheltering in his caring. Law clerks would soon adjust to a demanding schedule and be challenged to produce only their best. They would see, for instance, a several page dissent on which they had labored for days be cut in a matter of hours to a one-page masterpiece of legal clarity and conciseness. They would learn that every word needed to count. They would also discover on their trips out of town with the Judge that he possessed considerable physical stamina as well as a quick and incisive mind. One remembered an assignment in Washington on the D.C. Circuit Court of Appeals and staying at the Statler Hilton which was about a mile from the Federal Courthouse. "Each morning the Judge and I would walk up Pennsylvania Avenue to the Courthouse and each evening after a full day's work would walk home. The Judge meant business when he walked and would time us each morning. He always was delighted if we were able to cut a minute or two off our previous morning's walking time."[17]

The Washington assignments afforded the opportunity to keep in touch with old friends like Burton K. Wheeler. One of the most interesting evenings he had ever spent was at a dinner party at the Senator's home in 1968. Among the other guests was Senator James O. Eastland of Mississippi. Wheeler and Eastland reminisced about their experiences in the Senate and then began forecasting what would happen in the 1968 election. It was shortly before Bobby Kennedy's assassination in Los Angeles, but they were predicting that Vice President Hubert Humphrey would be the Democratic nominee and Richard Nixon the Republican choice. Then they predicted the outcome state by state, and proved to be right on every state except Texas.

Wheeler loved to tell stories as he ranged over one of the most influential careers in the history of Montana politics. He also had a keen sense of humor and was not above a practical joke, as evidenced by a story he told that evening. There was some legislation pending in the Senate in which Joseph Kennedy, a close personal friend, was interested and was endeavoring to get the support of Senator Langer of North Dakota. He arranged with Wheeler to invite Langer to the Kennedy residence for dinner. When Langer was unable to go, the resourceful Wheeler advised one of his staff members that he was to be the North Dakota senator for the occasion, knowing that Kennedy and Langer had not met. The party lasted late and Kennedy insisted that Wheeler and "Senator Langer" spend the night there, giving the latter the finest bedroom and red carpet treatment in all respects. It wasn't until a week later that Kennedy found out what had happened and conveyed his ire to Wheeler, who still thoroughly enjoyed what he had done.

At home, protracted litigation involving the construction of Yellowtail Dam on the Crow Indian Reservation occupied much of the Judge's time during his first years on the bench. His predecessor, Judge Pray, had held that the United States had authority to condemn lands owned by the members of the Crow Tribe and located on the Crow Indian Reservation for construction of the Yellowtail Dam and Reservoir on the Big Horn River. The Judge followed that ruling and held that water power value should be allowed in determining just compensation, and the Crow Tribe was not limited to what in effect would be a nominal value for grazing purposes. The court held further that in view of the complex situation presented the issue of just compensation should be determined by a commission rather than a jury, and the question of whether the Big Horn River was a navigable stream should be determined by the court.

Congress sought to resolve the question of the amount of just compensation, but the two legislative branches and the President were unable to agree upon the amount. A compromise was reached whereby $2,500,000 would be paid the Crow Indian Tribe and the Tribe would be permitted to sue in the Court of Claims or the District Court in Montana for additional compensation based on power site value. Following a protracted trial before the Judge, he concluded that just compensation for all of the tribal right, title, and interest was $4,500,000, resulting in an additional amount of $2,000,000 to the Tribe.

A case of far-reaching political consequences, which also took a lot of the Judge's time involved the legislative reapportionment issue. In 1962, the U.S. Supreme Court in *Baker v. Carr* ruled that a voter could challenge legislative apportionment on the grounds that it violated the equal protection clause of the Fourteenth Amendment. In *Reynolds v. Sims*, in 1964, the Court held that population (the one person-one vote principle) must be the primary consideration in apportioning state legislatures, that state assemblies must represent "people, not trees or acres" in districts "as nearly of equal population as practicable."

Legislative apportionment in Montana was based on both population and geography, so that each of the 56 counties was entitled to one and only one senator and, regardless of size, at least one representative. That meant that the 46 least populated counties numerically dominated the Senate, while approximately 40 per cent of the state's population elected a majority of the members of the House. When the new Legislature, in January of 1965, showed no inclination to follow the high court's ruling, a Butte voter brought suit in the case of *Herweg v. The Thirty-Ninth Legislative Assembly of the State of Montana.* District Judges Jameson and Murray and Circuit Judge Walter L. Pope comprised a three-judge court, which was disposed to give the assembly an opportunity to reapportion itself.

When adjournment came without such an effort having been made, the three judges issued their findings and decree in August. They found the provisions of the Montana Constitution and Code to be in violation of the Equal Protection Clause of the Fourteenth Amendment and ordered into effect a temporary and provisional plan of reapportionment of both houses and for use in the 1966 election. The Judge later remembered long hours spent in a Great Falls hotel room, calculator at hand, trying to figure out the population distribution of a legally constituted legislature.

The court-defined assembly was made up of 55 senators from 31 senatorial districts, combining counties where population considerations dictated, and 104 representatives from 38 districts likewise based on population features. When the Fortieth Assembly enacted the new provisions into law, the court proceeded in May of 1967 to issue its final order, holding the new reapportionment law to be valid and constituional and relinquishing any further jurisdiction. The result was a dramatic remapping of Montana's political landscape, with the larger counties figuring much more prominently in the legislative makeup.

Of the various cases brought into the Jameson court, one of his most significant and frequently cited decisions came in *Deeds v. United States.* Here the Government was held liable for injuries sustained by a 17 year old girl in an automobile accident, where Government employees had sold intoxicating liquor to the driver of the car, a minor intoxicated airman, knowing that he would have to drive his date home from the air base. At that time (1963), both the Montana statute and Air Force Regulations prohibited the sale of intoxicating liquor to intoxicated persons and persons under 21 years of age. The court found that the plaintiff was entitled to recover damages for the injuries received.

Judge Jameson (far right) with federal judges Walter L. Pope, George H. Boldt, and William D. Murray.

The quality of the Judge's work was recognized as early as 1961 when *Fortune Magazine* for December included him on its "Blue Ribbon Jury of American Judges." Six came from the federal bench and six from state and county courts. In *Fortune's* account: "The traditional heroes of the American bench write classic opinions and learned articles in law journals. But the indispensable colonels of today's battle for justice are the judges who have shown the way to efficient and skillful conduct of the trial courts. They work long hours and not only try cases but see that cases get to trial as fast as possible. With a twirl of the jury wheel *Fortune* has selected twelve representatives from a distinguished panel of this hardy breed. . ." With the picture of Judge Jameson, *Fortune* noted that at 63 "he has few backlogs in Montana, but has won respect for cleaning up court procedures."[18]

Fortune's estimate of the Judge's performance on the bench was sustained by his colleagues at home. "If one goes through the cases in the Montana State Reporter," one observed, "you won't find any authority I think cited more frequently, and with greater respect, that the decisions of Judge Jameson from the district bench here in Montana. Many a time. . . the Supreme Court of Montana, and other courts around the country, have examined the Judge's decisions and found them to have such tremendous logic, and such persuasion and such simplicity of approach, that they have virtually said, 'Gentlemen, this is the law.' "[19]

V.

The "efficient and skillful conduct" of his court did not keep the Judge from a continuing involvement with the A.B.A. and related organizations. He attended regularly the biannual sessions of the House of Delegates and shared actively in the Association's yearly meetings. He was at Miami Beach in August of 1959, when his good friend (and Bill, Jr.'s father-in-law) John D. Randall became president. Randall appointed him, along with Senators Bourke B. Hickenlooper of Iowa and John Stennis of Mississippi to a special committee to lay the foundation for the world-wide conference of lawyers.[20] Bill saw that as a significant means in furthering the hopes expressed at London for world peace through law.

Another particularly interesting assignment came in 1963 when he was attending the Annual Meeting in Chicago and was made Chairman of the A.B.A.'s Section of Judicial Administration. Notable during that year was the establishment of The National Judicial College for state court judges at the University of Nevada, Reno. The Fleischman Foundation had made a substantial grant available on condition that the college be located in Nevada. Bill was on the first board of directors and was with the majority in accepting the terms. During the next 20 years, some 13,000 judges from all 50 states and numerous foreign countries, would attend the College, taking courses ranging from one to four weeks and taught by leading legal scholars and practitioners. According to Chief Justice Warren E. Burger, Honorary Chairman of the College, "The national Judicial College is...one of the two most significant developments affecting the administration of justice in this century."[21]

In 1964 the soft-spoken, energetic jurist became involved in still another important project, which would have a very significant impact on the administration of justice in his own state. He became a member of the Advisory Council of the National Legal Aid and Defender Association. That move reflected his long-time interest in providing legal assistance for those unable to pay for services and representation for indigent persons accused of crimes. Happily, the Ford Foundation had made a grant of $2.3 million over a five year period for the National Defender Project, which was subsequently increased to $4.3 million. The basic objective of the Project was "to support a program of experiments to improve the administration of criminal justice by strengthening defender and auxiliary services required for defense of the accused in criminal cases."[22]

In no place was there a greater need for such a program than in his own state. Approximately 80% of the criminal cases in Montana's federal courts involved offenses arising on the seven widely scattered Indian reservations. In addition, there was the problem of jurisdictions, whether cases were to be handled in federal, state, or tribal courts. Over 95% of the Indians charged with crimes in federal court qualified for court appointed counsel. Unfortunately, few of the state's 900 practicing attorneys lived near the reservations and those who did were running as many as 10 to 15 appointments each year, with mostly Indian juveniles. The lawyers were in need of assistance in investigative and research work to insure

Directors of the Defender Project

an expeditious handling of the cases.

Such were the circumstances that led the Judge to seek the cooperation of Dean Robert E. Sullivan of the University of Montana Law School. With the full support of General Charles L. Decker, Director of the Project, the National Legal Aid and Defender Association approved in February, 1966 a three year grant of $54,150 to the Law School to establish a broad program, using law students to assist an assigned counsel in both the federal and state courts and to assist Indians and their tribal courts. Specifically, the program had four immediate objectives: "(1) to give senior law students practical experience in criminal law; (2) to meet the critical need to provide investigative and research services for counsel appointed to defend indigents, both Indian and non Indian; (3) to assist prison inmates with petitions for review of their convictions; and (4) to assist the tribal courts."[23]

The program was formally initiated on June 1, 1966 and by February of 1968 the Judge could write that it was an unqualified success. "The Montana Defender Project has demonstrated that a program of law school assistance in the defense of criminal cases may be conducted successfully in isolated areas at substantial distance from the law school. It is unique in that its primary objective is assistance in insuring an adequate representation for indigent Indians." The program was also accomplishing its purpose of stimulating the interest of participating students in the practice of criminal law. "The isolation of the classroom from the practice," one young lawyer wrote, "is particularly true in the criminal law and procedure field. Few law students have had any exposure to the segment of society from which criminal defendants, for the most part, originate or to the processes set up by society to deal with these persons. As a result criminal law, particularly criminal defense, is often looked upon by the graduate either with disdain or with a complete lack of interest. The Defender Project program has done a great deal to dispel this attitude and has created a real interest in criminal law among the students who have participated in it."[24]

For General Decker, as he reflected on the Judge's retirement from the active bench in 1969, there was "no living man who has done more for the legal profession and who has asked for less by way of recognition." He had in mind Bill's earlier assistance in establishing The Judge Advocate General's School at Charlottesville, Virginia and his role in the National Defender Project. "Through the efforts of Judge Jameson," he recalled, "the Montana Defender Project was established at the Law School, The University of Montana. The Montana Defender Project is now regarded as a model throughout the nation and has been copied at other law schools." Such contributions, the General observed, may "appear de minimus alongside his many broad-scale national contributions to the legal profession, but to millions of soldiers who have benefitted because of better legal service in the Army, to thousands of indigent defendants who have received competent representation, these achievements are major indeed."[25]

One other assignment of note involved the Judge in the nation's ongoing debate over the abolition of the Electoral College. President Johnson had revived the issue in messages to the Congress in 1965 and 1966, uring adoption of a Constitutional amendment to reform the Electoral College system. Congressional and executive leaders had requested that the A.B.A. undertake a study of the subject, in part, perhaps, because of the Association's help in promoting the Twenty-Fifth Amendment on Presidential Inability and the Vice-Presidential Vacancy.[26] In response, the Commission on Electoral College Reform was organized at the midyear session of the House of Delegates in February of 1966. The Judge joined a distinguished panel of governors, judges, lawyers, constitutional law authorities, political scientists, and representatives from labor and management. Following an indepth study, the Commission favored a more "truly democratic process" and concluded that it "seems most appropriate that the election of the nation's only two national officers be by national referendum."[27] The forces for the status quo, however, decreed that the debate would continue.

VI.

Another lively discussion of the times centered in the proper role of the U.S. Supreme Court, with critics charging that the Warren tribunal had widened unnecessarily the scope of judicial review and was deciding cases more on sociological than legal grounds. The Judge had an opportunity to reflect upon the controversy in an address before the Pacific Northwest Political Science Association. In his remarks, he was reminded of a recent series of lectures at Harvard Law School by Learned Hand, "one of the best legal minds and one of the ablest judges of this generation." In favoring a more limited scope of judicial review, the eminent jurist had said:

> Another supposed advantage of the wider power of review seems to be that by "the moral radiation of its decisions" a court may point the way to a resolution of the social conflicts involved better than any likely to emerge from a legislature. In other words, courts may light the way to a saner world and ought to be encouraged to do so. I should indeed be glad to believe it, and it may be that my failure hitherto to observe it is owing to some personal defect of vision; but at any rate judges have large areas left unoccupied by legislation within which to exercise this benign function. Besides, for a judge to serve as communal mentor appears to me a very dubious addition to his duties and one apt to interfere with their proper discharge.[28]

Obviously, not all of Judge Hand's contemporaries shared his views. The high court itself was divided, with its decisions reflecting basic differences in constitutional interpretation. On the fringes of the debate were the more strident critics, calling for a drastic curbing of the Court's powers. The Judge agreed with Senator Hennings of Missouri that "free and open criticism of the Court's decisions and opinions is healthy and desirable," but he deplored "any hasty or ill-considerd attempt to limit the powers of the Court by changing its basic structure." It seemed to him that a recent Law Day U.S.A. publication by the A.B.A. made a particularly pertinent observation:

> It is this capacity of the law to grow with the unfolding of the society it serves, as much as the wisdom of the Founding Fathers, which has given us the security of an enduring constitutional system. Of course, the growth of the law has not always been an orderly and logical process. The evidence of trial and error is voluminous. Sometimes judges have allowed superficial conclusions or ingrained habits of thought to obscure the fundamentals of a living Constitution. In these cases the courts have suffered what Chief Justice Hughes called "self-inflicted wounds." The important thing is that, in the long run, our system of free expression and independent courts has provided its own correctives. And, since the human mind can never be infallible, this may be as near to an ideal system as man can come.[29]

Aside from the debate over the Court, the Judge informed his hearers that the most important problem in the efficient administration of justice in the country was the law's delay. He was pleased to note the progress that had been made toward expediting the work of the courts. "There has been simplification of procedure through adoption of new rules, both cvil and criminal. It has been frequently said, and I think with justification, that the most significant reform and most far-reaching advance in Anglo-American Jurisprudence during the past fifty years has been the drastic simplification of judicial procedures in American courts."[30]

In June of 1964 the Judge gave a series of lectures at the Academy of American and International Law at Southwestern Legal Center, Dallas, in which he expanded upon his views of "Constitutional Law in the U.S." The sessions were attended by 40 registrants from 23 different countries. Meanwhile, the tensions of the 1960's found expression in a number of his speeches, including a commencement address at the College of Great Falls and a talk before the Billings Rotary Club.

For the graduates he had the admonition that "extremists on either side are rarely the guardians of human freedom. We must be careful also, whether we regard ourselves as conservatives or liberals, that our position is not determined by whose ox is being gored." Further, while we must protect individual rights, we must be "equally concerned with the correlative obligations of the individual to society. It is only through development of the public and individual sense of responsibility that nations and men become and remain free. The importance of wise restraints in the growth of human freedom is not limited to the field of law. It is the rule of life equally applicable in government, education, religion, the news media, as well as in our personal conduct and relationships one with another."[31] Nothing was closer to the marrow of the Judge's thinking than the wisdom of the balanced perspective or the use of healthy restraints, especially in a time that ran to excesses.

His speech before the Rotarians came at the end of a troubled 1968 and towards the close of one of the most turbulent decades in American history. Civil rights leader, Martin Luther King, Jr., had been slain in Memphis in early April. Democratic presidential contender, Robert Kennedy, openly shared the outrage and grief of Black America, only himself to fall before the assassin's bullet in early June. Alienation over Vietnam shadowed the land and the Great Society was not to be. Never, perhaps, was a topic more timely than that of the Judge's discussion of "Civil Disobedience and the Right of Dissent."

He had been on court assignment in Washington shortly after Dr. King was shot, had witnessed the rioting and the rise of Resurrection City. Housed in a hotel on Massachusetts Avenue at the beginning of Embassy Row, he was still strongly cautioned against walking out after dark. The dangers of lawlessness were such in many cities that Mr. Justice Fortas in a speech before the American College of Trial Lawyers wondered if the people of the country still accepted, as an article of faith and the basic scheme of the Constitution, the duty to obey the law.

A nation on edge, buffeted by various protests, had helped the Judge to crystallize his thinking on a most complicated problem. The difference, for him, was clear between civil disobedience and dissent, with the first involving "deliberate and open violation of any law which an individual or group believed to be unjust with a view toward effecting its change." Dissent or protest, by contrast, were lawful means of disagreement "protected by the First Amendment...and are essential to the democratic form of government."[32]

Direct civil disobedience (violating the law one is protesting), in the Judge's view, was "in some instances. . .justified in order to test the constitutionality of a particular law. When a person feels that a statute violates his constitutional rights, he should always in my opinion be permitted to test in the courts the validity of that law. Sometimes this may be done only by violating the questionable law. In that event, if the trial court finds the act valid, ordinarily a nominal fine is imposed and appeal taken. If there is some other means of testing the validity of the law, that means should of course be followed."

The appeal to moral right to civil disobedience provided the most controversy. American jurists, the Judge noted, like Chief Justice Hughes had long held that, "in the forum of conscience, duty to a moral power higher than the State has always been maintained." Yet, the "duty to the State exists within the domain of power, for government may enforce obedience to laws regardless of scruples. When one's belief collides with the power of the State, the latter is Supreme within its sphere and submission or punishment follows." As Alexander Hamilton pointed out in the *Federalist Papers*, "If there be no penalty annexed to disobedience, the resolutions or command which pretend to be laws will, in fact, amount to nothing more than advice or recommendation." The Judge quoted Dean Erwin Griswold in urging that decisions to violate the law for moral reasons "should be made only after the most painful and introspective reflection, and only when the firm conclusion is reached that obedience offends the most fundamental personal value." It must be recognized also that society not only does not but can not grant the moral right to disobey the law as entitled to legal privilege.

In drawing a distinction between lawful dissent and unlawful civil disobedience, the Judge quoted Earl Morris, immediate

A.B.A. past president, to illustrate the point:

"When a group of college students marches on the campus in orderly, peaceful fashion carrying antiwar signs, or when a university faculty member writes a paper criticizing the legality of the American position in Vietnam, this is dissent—legal, constitutional, protected by the First Amendment. But when students obstruct the work of interviewers representing the Central Intelligence Agency, the Armed Forces, and certain private corporations, or when students storm the Vice President of the United States in his car, hit the windows and body of the car with their fists and shout obscenities, this is civil disobedience in its most virulent form—and it is unlawful. . . .

What is reprehensible in these acts is not the point of view, not the end to be achieved—one may or may not agree with them—but the methods of achieving them. A clergyman has the right to voice his dissent to the Vietnam War from his pulpit, but it is different thing when he becomes a part of a group preventing inductees from entering an induction center. I would ask that clergyman how he would react if, on a Sunday morning, an antireligious group blocked the entrance to his church and prevented his parishioners from entering."

Judge Jameson, Mildred, Mother and Lucille

The danger implicit in civil disobedience was to condone a general disregard for law and to suggest that each citizen has a right to determine for himself which laws are just and which shall be obeyed. That really amounted to denying the rule of law as the governing yardstick of society's conduct. Such disregard, it should be noted, was not limited to violent protests in the streets, but also was to be found in dishonest business practices or wherever callous attitudes made for lower standards of behavior. Let us be vigorous, the Judge concluded, "in expressing our dissent and pursuing any lawful means to change specific laws or governmental policy we consider unjust, but let us do so without violence or lawlessness—in accordance with law and not in defiance of law. Likewise, let us grant to other persons the right of vigorous dissent and protest, but let us give our full support to the law enforcement officers and college administrators who insist that the right of dissent be exercised without violence or rioting and in full compliance with the law."

VII.

The 1960's were also an eventful time for the Jameson family. They opened with Annie's passing and closed with Bill's retirement from the active judgeship. Midway there would be the pain of loss with Walker Honaker's untimely death, bringing a new way of life for Mary and the children. But Bill, Jr. and wife Sue would add two grandchildren to Mary's five, so the family was both diminished and imbued with new life. Whatever the satisfactions of a very rewarding career, it was in the circle of family and home that Bill Jameson's domestic nature found contentment and joy to round out the meaning of his days.

Annie's health had been failing for several years. Blood pressure problems had kept her from being at Bill, Jr.'s wedding in 1953. Fortunately, a new drug Reserpine was available and helpful so that she could be in Chicago for the A.B.A. meeting, to share that high moment of hopes fulfilled with her son, though there was a sadness that Will was not with her. By late 1959 she had developed pernicious anemia and stomach cancer and Reserpine had lost its effectiveness. Three strokes followed in January of 1960 but failed to dim the light of her spirit. Frail of body, as she lay on the couch, she filled her days with singing. Remarkably, her voice was still strong.

Bill and Mildred, Mary and the children were there for her last birthday on June 4th—and she was overjoyed. It was a time for recollection of a lifetime together, of love given and received, and as the memories flowed there was also the laughter. Good humor was a real part of the celebration of a life that had been truly enjoyed. She died on August 23 in her 85th year.

Most of her generation were gone, but there were the letters of affection deeply felt from friends of former times. An old Roundup acquaintance wrote: "Everyone in Roundup looked up to her as very special." And another: "Every memory of her is precious and joyous." And from her doctor: "She was one of the sweetest, no, I believe the very sweetest person I have ever known." In her life of loving and caring, of daily Bible reading and silent prayer, she had been living in the presence of her God. So the Reverend Hugh Herbert put it wisely in his funeral sermon—she had just gone through an open door.

Walker Honaker had established a private medical practice, located in the duplex Will had built. He and Mary saw their family grow to five: Kathy, Liz and Jim, Bill and Bob. The Judge and Mildred were frequent visitors at the busy home on Parkhill Drive, where he could be found on the floor playing with the children and their toys. In 1965 the grandparents took the three older children on a trip to Disneyland. Mary and Walker were to follow a few days later with the two youngest. He had a heart attack while trying to save a coronary victim. After three weeks in the hospital and a few weeks at home, he felt able to travel with Mary to Seattle for a vacation on Whidby Island. On the way, however, at Kellogg, Idaho, he had a massive cerebral hemorrhage and died.

As a part of grief's slow wisdom, Mary returned to school and earned her baccalaureate degree in nursing from Montana State University. She then pursued her profession in Billings with School District 2. Bill and Mildred helped her with the parenting, easing in ways they could the burden of loss for mother and children. Mary found meaning and healing for the spirit in sharing herself with others, turning her garage into a clearing house of clothes, food, and household articles, which she then distributed to those in need. For her habit of "walking the second mile," she was recognized in 1970 as "Woman of the Year" by the Billings Business and Professional Women's Club.

Bill Jr.'s educational career had taken him from Missoula to the University of Texas, where he earned the M.A. in Physics in 1954. Later, in 1962, he was awarded the Ph.D. in Mathematics by Iowa State University. During his time with the Air Force (1952-1958), he had served as a Nuclear Research Officer and as Director in Administrative Services. Following a year at Lockheed Missiles and Space Company, he taught part-time at Iowa State University and (beginning in 1962) joined the Collins Radio Company. Children Margaret Elizabeth and Katharine Rebecca came along in 1967 and 1970. Bill's work would keep him in Iowa, but his roots remained deep in his Montana childhood.

As the decade was ending and he crossed over his seventieth year, the Judge weighed his options—to enter retirement or to take senior status. The latter meant working at least half time, retaining a secretary and a law clerk, and sitting on cases within and outside the state. It was really not a difficult decision for one who loved the law and whose life had centered so much in the routine of work. His decision to take senior status was made in early February of 1969 and prompted the *Gazette* to editorialize that Montana and the nation were fortunate that he had decided to stay on the bench. "Few men in his profession have garnered the honors that came, over his long career in law, to William J. Jameson—and few have worn them as unassumingly or as graciously. For it is in men such as him that the phrase 'with justice for all' takes and holds meaning for citizens who have recourse to the courts of our land."[33]

CHAPTER EIGHT

THE SENIOR CIRCUIT

Few events in the city's history produced a greater flow of telegrams and letters from high places. It was Wednesday, June 11, 1969, and the Yellowstone County Bar Association was honoring its most illustrious member on the occasion of his retirement from the active federal judgeship. Over 400 guests from around the state came in for the Testimonial Dinner. William T. Gossett of Detroit, current president of the A.B.A., was there to deliver the main address. Billings artist-lawyer, James M. Haughey, had painted for the program a portrait of his long-time friend and associate in the law.

Chief Justice Earl Warren wired his appreciation for the Judge's "splendid work as a member of the federal judiciary," Associate Justice Tom C. Clark thanked him for "a career of untiring devotion to justice and to humanity," former Attorney General Herbert Brownell remembered that the Judge's appointment to the federal bench had given President Eisenhower particular pleasure, and A.B.A. Past President Charles S. Rhyne characterized his friend as "one of the all-time greats of the legal profession." These and other leaders in law, government, and business joined in expressing a deep-felt "well-done."

Yellowstone Bar President, Frank A. Gallagher, observed that the Judge's "probity and his wisdom will long be an inspiration to the lawyers of Montana." Then to correct a longstanding oversight on motion by Frederic Moulton, he ruled that the Judge's name be inscribed by acclamation on the Association's role as President Emeritus. That took care of the one office that he had missed in not heading the county bar.

Federal Judge Russell E. Smith of Missoula said of his long-time friend: "If I were to make an image of the federal judiciary, I would make it in the image of Bill Jameson." President Gossett spoke of the Judge's outstanding contributions on the national scene and remarked that the occasion was "abundant testimony of the affection which Montana holds for a man of such compassion and such wisdom."[1] The *Gazette's* Addison Bragg, in his "Such Interesting People" column, noted a day or two earlier that with all of his accomplishments and recognitions the Judge remained free of pretentiousness or pomposity. His customary response on the phone was still: "Hello—this is Bill Jameson." Mildred wondered in a letter to Lucille if he were not too modest; yet, "it's one of his most 'valuable traits'! It's one of the reasons he's so universally loved and respected by the bar."

The very pleasant evening at the Northern signified another milestone, but his journey with the law was far from over. In that, too, his many friends found reason to rejoice.

II.

There were other considerations than love of work and the law that led the Judge to take senior status. He thoroughly enjoyed his associations in the federal judiciary and looked forward to sitting with other jurists on the several courts of appeal. There were the opportunities to work with great legal minds like Learned Hand and to enjoy unforgettable personalities like Harold Medina. In the years ahead, he would sit on six of the twelve circuit courts in the nation and also on the Temporary Emergency Court of Appeals. The latter tribunal was created to handle cases arising under the Economic Stabilization Act of 1971 and would become concerned almost exclusively with litigation involving the Department of Energy and various categories of oil companies.

Another compelling reason he shared with other senior judges was to help with the tremendous increase in the volume of court work brought on by the "litigation explosion." Chief Justice Burger would later report that from 1940 to 1981 annual federal district civil case filings increased from about 35,000 to 180,000, almost doubling the yearly case load per judgeship from 190 to 350 cases. The increase was nearly six times that of population growth! Even more startling were the annual court of appeals filings, which would soar from 2,800 in 1950 to over 26,000 in 1981, with an increase in annual case load per circuit judgeship from 44 to 200 cases, or a growth rate sixteen times that of the population!

Aside from the general trends toward an increasingly litigious society, with more and more people suing each other over a wide assortment of grievances, two factors in particular were crowding the federal courts. First, there was a tremendous surge in prisoner petitions, both at the state and federal levels, with repeated appeals consuming a great deal of time. Second, new legislation concerning Civil Rights, freedom of information, truth in lending, and numerous regulatory statutes, while generally desirable, were creating serious problems for the courts when Congress failed to provide the necessary personnel to do the work.

Further, abuse of legislation contributed to court congestion. The Freedom of Information Act of 1966 (strengthened by amendments in 1974) was a good example, resulting frequently in prolonged and complex cases. The law required federal agencies to make information available to journalists and other persons, unless it fell into one of several exempted and confidential categories. All too often, however, it was being used by people charged with serious offenses as a means of discovering what evidence the Government might have against them. The Judge, for instance, would sit on one case in the Seventh Circuit in Chicago, where the defendant sought all documents and papers regarding him in the hands of four different agencies, namely, the F.B.I., Customs Service, Treasury Department (Bureau of Alcohol, Tobacco and Firearms), and the Secret Service. Each agency had furnished a substantial number of documents and several thousand pages of records, but had excised some material, particularly the names of persons furnishing the information and had refused a few documents. All of the refused material had been submitted to a district judge for *in camera* inspection. He had found that they were properly refused under the exemption provisions of the Act, and the circuit judges upheld his decision.

The federal judiciary, then, badly needed the senior judges, and the jurist from Montana was not at all loath to oblige. At home, he soon found himself involved in another round of reapportionment problems. State Representative Thomas E. Towe and others had brought suit in the U.S. District Court in Billings, charging that the new reapportionment law of 1971 violated the one-man, one-vote principle. In early June of 1971, Federal Judges James R. Browning, William J. Jameson, and Russell E. Smith found the statute to be unconstitutional in providing for impermissable variations in legislative district populations. By November of that year, however, the same judicial panel could uphold a revised plan adopted by a special legislative session, providing for 50 senators and 100 representatives in 23 districts covering the state's electorate. "We concluded," the panel wrote, "that the legislative assembly made a good faith effort to comply as nearly as practical with the one-man, one-vote principle."[2]

An equally momentous decision involved the state's new constitution. In March of 1973 the Montana Farm Bureau Federation had filed its third suit against the new document, which had been approved very narrowly (116,415 to 113,883) by the voters the previous June. In August of 1972, the Montana Supreme Court had upheld the new constitution in a 3-2 decision, and the following February the U.S. Supreme Court had rejected an appeal without explanation. The third suit then was filed in March in the District Court, contending that 7,302 voters had been misled by state officials. Federal Judges James R. Browning, William J. Jameson, and William D. Murray, meeting in Missoula on June 27, dismissed the suit "with prejudice," thereby prohibiting the Farm Bureau from filing another lawsuit for the same reasons in that court. So the new constitution survived its third court test, replaced its 84-year-old predecessor, and went into effect three days later, on July 1. Relieved supporters had wondered about the status of many laws passed in implementation of the new frame of state government—had the judicial panel decided otherwise.

Considerable court time for the Judge in Montana would be taken with Indian litigation. In 1972 he was confronted with a case of major significance to the Northern Cheyennes. The Northern Cheyenne Allotment Act of 1926 provided that the timber, coal, and other minerals on the Reservation were to be reserved for the benefit of the Tribe for fifty years or until 1976, when they should become the property of the allottees or their heirs.

In 1968, before the expiration of the fifty years, Congress passed an act reserving the timber, coal, and other minerals in perpetuity for the benefit of the Tribe and authorized the Tribe to commence an action in the District Court of Montana "to determine whether under (the 1926 Act) the allottees, their heirs, or devisees, have received a vested property right in the minerals which is protected by the fifth amendment." The Judge concluded that, "consistent with Congressional policy and comparable allotment acts reserving minerals to a tribe, the Northern Cheyenne Allotment Act of June 3, 1926, also reserves sufficient power in the Congress to reserve the Northern Cheyenne mineral estate ' in perpetuity for the benefit of the tribe,' and that the allottees, their heirs and devisees, received no 'vested property right in the minerals which is protected by the fifth amendment.' "[3]

The Court of Appeals reversed this decision, but the U.S. Supreme Court agreed with the district court in a ruling handed down in May of 1976. The high tribunal held that the 1926 Act did not give the allottees of surface lands vested rights in the mineral deposits underlying those lands and that Congress had not intended to "relinquish control and management. . . as Congress may deem expedient for the Indians." On the Reservation, according to the *Billings Gazette*, there was both "delight" and "despair." Those who hailed the Court's decision agreed that the coal reserves belonged to all and that mineral development would be more orderly in tribal hands. But disappointed allottees claimed that they had been denied their individual property rights.

Meanwhile, in March of 1974, the Judge became involved in a particularly interesting case in Missoula which involved Indian claims to the south half of Flathead Lake. For decades the Confederated Salish and Kootenai Tribes had been urging their ownership of the lake bed and banks, in accordance with their understanding of the Treaty of Hell Gate of 1855, which located that part of the lake within their Reservation. Lakeshore property owners had been countering with their rights to lake water.

The Tribes brought suit in the District Court when the owner of Jim's Marina at Polson began building a breakwater on lakeshore property he had acquired from an Indian allottee. The Tribes contended that the Treaty established as their property everything below the high water mark, and they wanted payment for use of their water. The defense, representing other lakeshore property owners as well as Jim's Marina (and with the City of Polson as an interested party), argued that they had "riparian rights," that is, legal access to the bed and banks of the lake for such uses as bathing, drinking, watering stock, and irrigation.

In a 23-page decision, the Judge found that the lake bed and banks fell under the jurisdiction of the federal government, not tribal law. He concluded that from the long history of navigation on the lake that riparian lands under the Indian Allotment Acts carried the rights of access and wharfage. He wrote that granting the Indians' claim "would be a grievous injustice to the defendants and others in a similar position." He found "the defendants as owners of lands riparian to the south half of Flathead Lake are entitled as a matter of law to access to the lake. Concomitant with that right of access is the right to wharf out of navigable water."[4]

The question remained open as to whether or not the marina's dock and other structures represented an abuse of riparian rights and he instructed both parties to submit briefs on that issue. The Tribes, however, had already indicated their intention to appeal. The Ninth Circuit Court of Appeals acted in May of the following year, confirming the judgement against their claims. The U.S. Supreme Court, in November of 1976, refused to entertain a further appeal.

In subsequent proceedings Judge Jameson ruled that the Tribes had no right to regulate the riparian rights of non-Indian owners of land within the Flathead Reservation. This portion of his opinion was reversed by the Ninth Circuit, the court holding that the Tribe had a right to apply its ordinance in regulating all riparian rights on the south half of Flathead Lake, including those of non-Indian land owners.

The Flathead Tribes were also involved in litigation with the State Department of Revenue and others concerning the state cigarette tax and personal property taxes, particularly automobile taxes. They claimed exemption based on the Hell Gate Treaty of 1855. The three-judge panel of Browning, Jameson, and Smith heard the cigarette tax petition in May of 1974 and ruled in a two to one decision that the Indians could sell untaxed cigarettes within the Reservation to other Indians, but not to non-Indians without a tax. This decision was reaffirmed in February of 1975, and the judges also ruled that the Tribes did not have to pay motor vehicle property taxes. The State appealed and the next year the high court upheld the decision that Montana may not impose its cigarette and personal property taxes on the Indians of the Flathead Reservation.

State revenues also figured in a case which was of particular interest to Montana's hunters. At issue was the considerable disparity between resident and nonresident elk licenses, with the contention of the out-of-staters that this violated the privileges and immunites clause of the equal protection clause of the U.S. Constitution. The Judge sat on another three-judge panel that found, in a two to one decision, nothing unconstitutional in the license requirement. The case was appealed and in mid-1978 the Supreme

Court upheld the ruling. The high tribunal found "no irrationality in the differences the Montana Leigslature has drawn in the costs of its licenses to hunt elk. The legislative choice was an economic means not unreasonably related to the preservation of a finite resource and a substantial regulatory interest of the state."[5]

The Judge's performance in these and other cases in Montana was rated high by the legal profession. On December 2, 1977, the *Great Falls Tribune* reported survey results of lawyers practicing in federal courts in the state for the previous three years. Of the 423 attorneys contacted, 46 per cent participated. The five areas of evaluation were: impartiality, judicial temperament, legal ability, diligence, and overall evaluation. He scored highest in judicial temperament and legal ability and had a near-perfect approval rate of 96 per cent in the overall evaluation.

While the Montana work produced a number of interesting cases, more of his time was taken with assignments in appellate courts around the country. Here, two were particularly notable for their complexity and international ramifications. The so-called *Zeiss Case* in 1970 involved the ownership and use in this country of Zeiss names and marks on optical and mechanical precision instruments. The plaintiffs were the Carl Zeiss *Stifftung* (or Foundation) located in Heidenheim, West Germany, and its subsidiary in Stuttgard. The defendants were the VEB ('Peoples Owned Enterprise'), Carl Zeiss Jena, situated in East Germany and two of its distributors in the United States. Each claimed the right to exclusive use of the trademarks as successor of the original Carl Zeiss Foundation established in Jena in 1889. It was not a charitable entity, but a private foundation for the purpose of owning and operating the Zeiss optical business (first organized in 1846) for profit. By 1945 the Foundation had acquired interests in numerous other commercial enterprises.

Problems for Zeiss began with the division of Germany after Hitler's fall. When it was determined that Jena would be in the Soviet Zone, American military authorities evacuated all management personnel (and top scientific and production people) of the Zeiss firms to Heidenheim in the U.S. Zone. There they built a factory to assist in the continuing war effort against Japan. Zeiss management designated three employees to carry on at Jena during their absence. Shortly, the occupying Soviets sequestered the assets of the firm as reparations, the plants having been used in the war effort. Zeiss in Jena was almost totally dismantled, but, later, the plant was partially rebuilt.

In 1954 the Zeiss Foundation in Heidenheim brought an action in the West German courts against Zeiss VEB, seeking an injunction against the use of the Zeiss trade names and marks. The trial court ruled favorably and the decision was later upheld by the Federal Supreme Court of West Germany in July of 1957. In the meantime, the Supreme Court of East Germany had ruled in favor of the Jena group. The case, involving use of the trademarks in the United States, was argued in the U.S. District Court for the Southern District of New York, where, after a six-week trial, it was determined that the West German Foundation was the true Zeiss Foundation. Following at least a month of pouring over all of the evidence, the U.S. Court of Appeals, Second Circuit, upheld the lower court's ruling. Judge Jameson recalled that his summary of the 180 findings of fact of the trial judge took over ten printed pages. The *Zeiss Case* was one that he would long remember.

Much better known to the public at large were the *Iranian Cases* of 1981. In May of that year, the Judge had accepted an assignment to the Court of Appeals for the District of Columbia. Shortly before leaving Billings, he was notified by the chairman of his panel that they would have two of the Iranian cases on their calendar. He was to be in Washington for parts of two weeks and had planned to spend the weekend with friends. Instead, he had to use that time huddled with some twenty briefs that had been filed by various banks and businesses, the Islamic Republic of Iran, various agencies of the Iranian Government, Iranian banks, and the United States Government as an intervenor. Fortunately, he remembered, the cases proved to be very interesting.

The background, of course, was the seizure of the American Embassy in Teheran on November 4, 1979 and the taking of its personnel as hostages. On advice that Iran intended to withdraw all assets from United States banks, President Carter moved on November 14 to sign an order, subsequently implemented by Treasury regulations, freezing all Iranian funds that "are in or come within the possession of control of persons subject to the jurisdiction of the United States."[6] This was followed on November 26 with the granting of a general license authorizing judicial proceedings against Iran. The President also issued an order that all such regulations could be amended or revoked at any time. Eventually over 400 suits, involving claims of three to four billion dollars, were filed against Iran and Iranian entities and were scattered among 35 federal district and 5 circuit courts. One claim reached the Supreme Court.

These cases were pending when the United States and the Islamic Republic of Iran agreed on terms for the release of the hostages on January 19, 1981. With the Algerian Government acting as mediator, the two countries agreed to terminate all litigation between the government of each party and the nationals of the other and to bring about the settlement and resolution of all such claims through binding arbitration. To that end, the agreement provided for the establishment of an *Iran-United States Claims Tribunal*, composed of at least nine members, one-third to be selected by the United States, one-third by Iran, and the remaining one-third by the other members. The tribunal was to arbitrate any claims not settled within six months and its awards were to be "final and binding" and enforceable in the courts of any nation.

The agreement provided further: (1) for the termination of all legal proceedings in the United States involving claims of United States persons against Iran and its state enterprises; (2) to nullify all attachments and judgments; (3) to bring about the transfer by July 19, 1981 of all Iranian assets in this country by American banks, except that (4) one billion dollars of these assets were to be deposited in a security account in the bank of England, to the account of the Algerian Central Bank and used to satisfy awards rendered against Iran by the Claims Tribunal. President Carter issued a series of orders on January 19, 1981 implementing the terms of the agreement and on February 24 President Reagan issued his order ratifying the agreement.

In the case which reached the Supreme Court, the plaintiff contended that the actions of the President and the Secretary of the Treasury were beyond their statutory and constitutional powers. At issue were three specific executive actions involving the power of the President: (1) to nullify judicial attachments; (2) to order the transfer of Iranian assets; (3) to suspend claims against Iran pending in United States courts. In each instance, the high court found grounds for sustaining the President's actions.

Of interest, too, were the Judge's assignments on the Temporary Emergency Court of Appeals. The Court normally sat in panels of three judges in different parts of the country, as the need arose. The cases almost entirely concerned the Department of Energy and various categories of oil companies. His work on this tribunal was of such merit that Chief Judge of the Court, Edward Allen Tamm of Washington, D.C., wrote to him in December 15, 1978:

My dear Bill:

I am tremendously impressed with the brillance of your

outstanding opinion in the Oil Company cases (16 cases were consolidated on appeal) and extend to you my sincere congratulations. Both the breadth and the depth of your research and treatment of these difficult problems reflect credit not only on our court, but upon the entire judiciary. Already the press is carrying extensive articles on these rulings.

This court and its judges are most fortunate in having the benefit of your participation in the court's deliberations and responsibilities.

III.

Along with the challenges and compensations of the Senior Circuit, the Judge continued his longstanding involvement with the A.B.A. Most notably, he was in the vanguard of the Association's efforts to develop standards for the administration of criminal justice in the country. For years each Annual Meeting had produced its testimony of the necessity for such an endeavor. At Chicago in 1954, it will be remembered, Associate Justice Jackson had noted that "dissatisfaction with our criminal law and administration mounts daily," that the "need for overhauling our criminal procedures is apparent in each day's news."[7] That was really the beginning of a serious consideration of the matter within the A.B.A.

By 1963 the Association, in conjunction with the Institute of Judicial Administration, was ready to formulate a project. At that time, the Judge was serving as chairman of the A.B.A.'s Section of Judicial Administration and so would be centrally involved. The Institute conducted a pilot study in the spring of 1964 and concluded that a project was feasible to formulate minimum standards in the field of criminal justice. It was then approved by the Board of Governors and the House of Delegates at the Annual Meeting in August and financing was obtained. New A.B.A. President, Lewis F. Powell, Jr., appointed the necessary committees, composed of federal and state judges, prosecutors, public defenders, practicing lawyers, law school professors and deans, and enforcement and correction officials.

The project was to embrace the full spectrum of the criminal processes from arrest through trial and appellate review. Its general purpose was described as:

> A major effort of the nation's organized bar, this project is attempting to compile and formulate standards which can be recommended as a desirable minimum to be applied to the administration of criminal justice in all of the 50 states and, when appropriate, through the jurisdiction of the federal government. The underlying objectives are two-fold: to promote effective law enforcement and the adequate protection of the public and to safeguard and amplify the constitutional rights of those suspected of crime.[8]

The study was first headed (1963-1968) by Judge J. Edward Lumbard of the Court of Appeals for the Second Circuit and then by Judge Warren E. Burger (1968-1969) of the U.S. Court of Appeals for the District of Columbia. When President Nixon named Burger to the Supreme Court in 1969, Judge Jameson became chairman of the Special Committee. Meanwhile, the word "minimum" was dropped from the description of the project's objectives, in favor of "desirable" or "acceptable" standards. What had been envisioned as a three-year undertaking was soon seen as of longer duration. The last of the several standards would not be ready for adoption by the House of Delegates until August of 1972, just eight years after the project was authorized.

In presenting the Second Edition of the A.B.A. Standards to the Montana Supreme Court, the Judge recalled that he had spent the equivalent of ten months on the project during the period from 1963 to 1973. "There was extensive research, discussion and debate before the Standards were finally approved. Quite naturally the prosecutors did not always agree with defense counsel and often the judges and law professors did not agree with either. Sometimes it seemed the viewpoints were in hopeless conflict. Yet with rare exceptions, through extensive debate, sometimes heated and protracted, the committee members were able to agree upon a satisfactory compromise fair to both society and the accused." He felt that the Chief Justice aptly summarized the results: "The drafters of these standards would not make claim to their perfection in any sense. Of necessity many of the standards reflect the traditional compromise of any delibertative process...I doubt that any one of the one hundred lawyers, judges, and law professors who worked on the project agreed with every standard on every subject, but taken as a whole (they) represent the richest source ever developed to bring the administration of criminal justice up to date."[9]

Of the fifteen standards which had been approved through 1971, the most controversial by far dealt with electronic

Presentation American Bar Association Medal, 1973.

surveillance. The heated debate within the A.B.A., at the Midyear Meeting in Chicago, February, 1971, reflected the sharp division of views in the country at large. Opponents of legalized wiretapping contended that the right of privacy was being increasingly eroded by the sophisticated listening devises of the technological age. Proponents, including prosecutors and law enforcement officials, defended the use of "the uninvited ear" (Justice Potter Stewart's phrase) as a necessary tool in coping with espionage and organized crime. In the "law and order" mood of the late 1960's, Congress passed (1968) the Omnibus Crime Control and Safe Streets Act, permitting court-authorized wiretapping in a range of cases.

The House of Delegates endorsed the federal wiretapping law as written 127 to 104, with three former A.B.A. presidents urging support of the measure. Judge Jameson joined Lewis F. Powell, Jr. and Ross L. Malone in arguing that such a law was needed as "guidance to the state legislatures. Many of the bills being considered in the legislatures are less restrictive than this."[10] With regard to the Standards generally, their completion would be seen as one of the A.B.A.'s most monumental accomplishments — one in which the judge from Montana had had a major leadership role!

The Standards were well received by the bench and the bar throughout the country. The Judge could observe in 1980 that already "they have been cited more than 8,000 times by state and federal courts, including almost 100 citations in decisions of the Supreme Court of the United States." Following the completion of

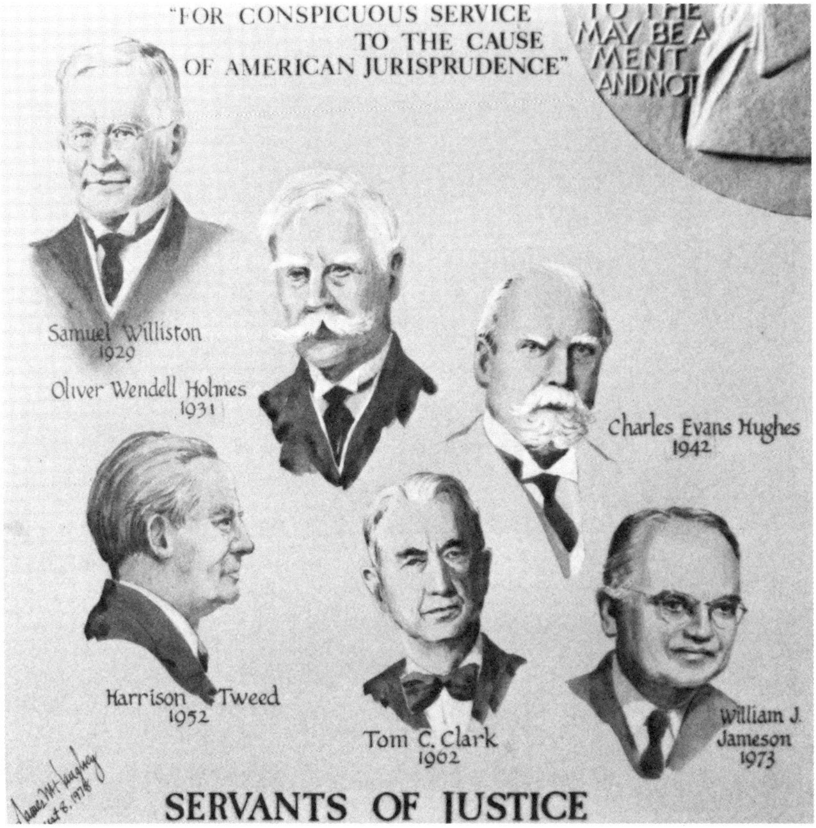
"FOR CONSPICUOUS SERVICE
TO THE CAUSE
OF AMERICAN JURISPRUDENCE"
Samuel Williston
1929
Oliver Wendell Holmes
1931
Charles Evans Hughes
1942
Harrison Tweed
1952
Tom C. Clark
1962
William J. Jameson
1973
SERVANTS OF JUSTICE

Recipients American Bar Association Medal, Painting by James M. Haughey.

THE AMERICAN BAR ASSOCIATION MEDAL

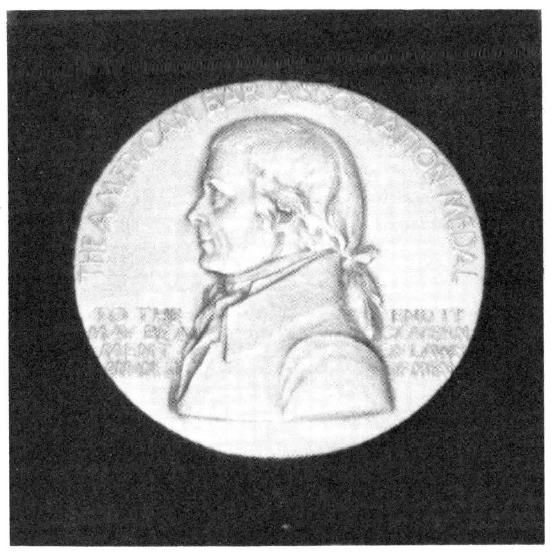

American Bar Association Medal, 1973.

the initial project in 1973, various task forces continued to review and recommend changes in the Standards in the light of court decisions and statutory enactments.

His contribution to this very important undertaking, along with many others to the Association and to the legal profession at large, was recognized at the 96th Annual Meeting in Washington in August of 1973. He became the thirty-eighth recipient of the American Bar Association medal, awarded for "conspicuous service in the cause of American jurisprudence." He joined an illustrious company which included Elihu Root (1930), Oliver

The American Judicature Society

Presents its

Herbert Lincoln Harley Award

to

William J. Jameson

in recognition of services in promoting

The Efficient Administration of Justice

as

lawyer, legislator and judge in his home state; without peer in his dedication to improving justice in Montana and nationally; as president of the American Bar Association, American Bar Endowment and the Montana Bar Association; chairman of innumerable state and national bar committees concerned with judicial administration and with establishing standards for the administration of criminal justice; and as director and president of the American Judicature Society.

June 1, 1974

The American Judicature Society to promote the Efficient Administration of Justice

Wendell Holmes (1931), Roscoe Pound (1940), Charles Evans Hughes (1942), Tom C. Clark (1962), and Felix Frankfurter (1963). In his citation, President Robert W. Meserve stated:

> It is said that law is a public profession. The tradition of service and leadership which supports that profession is nowhere better illustrated than in the career of Judge William J. Jameson. He is without peer in his dedication to his community, his native state of Montana, the organized bar and, above all, to the unending search for justice itself. He has brought honor to the profession and it is fitting that he be honored with the American Bar Association Medal, the Association's highest award...
>
> Judge Jameson has earned the respect of members of the bar and of the public by hard work and uncompromising integrity. He is known as a thoughtful man, a man of judicial temperament and grace, a man who has made immeasurable contributions to his profession and society. Daniel Webster said: "Justice, Sir, is the greatest interest of man here on Earth." William J. Jameson as lawyer, legislator, leader of the bar and judge has lived these words.[11]

The Judge's contributions in improving the administration of justice received further recognition the following year by the American Judicature Society. The Society's Herbert Lincoln Hartley Award, named for its founder, was presented to him by Dean Robert E. Sullivan of the Law School at the annual meeting of the Montana Bar Association. The Award honors judges, lawyers or laymen "who have made outstanding contributions to court modernization and reform in their state."[12]

IV.

Senior status had brought little relaxation in his routine. Work was still at the heart of his life. He continued to arrive at his office by 7:30 A.M., having walked part of the way from home. Enroute he would have been picked up by Thelma L. Green, his secretary since 1963. From then until 4 P.M. or so, she and a succession of law clerks would try to keep pace with the energetic judge. Coffee breaks were not in his scheme of things and lunch was often at the cafeteria in the Federal Building, where he took only time enough to eat his meal. His law clerk remembered that when the Judge was vacating his chambers for his successor on the active bench, Judge James F. Battin, he never missed an hour of work![13]

He still packed briefcases with books and judicial matters when he left for a weekend at Camp Senia. The few vacation trips he took were somehow combined with business. Only once, Mildred recalled, was she able to get her husband to leave the briefcases home, when they took a leisure cruise along the Alaskan coast. His idea of stewardship also included the resources within his public trust. When he traveled on business, he never went first class at the people's expense!

He still found time to accommodate the requests for speeches, at service clubs, on Law Days, at colleges and universities, and on various other occasions. He was always glad to appear on a campus, to stay in touch with higher education which had held his interest across the years. College teaching, he reflected, would have been his second career choice. In addition to continuing close associations with the University and Law School in Missoula, he served on the Board of Trustees at Rocky Mountain College from which he had received an honorary degree. It was there, at a Founders Day Banquet on May 31, 1969, that he delivered some thoughts on "Those Wise Restraints Which Make Men Free."

It was an interesting topic for the ending of a troubled decade. The 1960's had swelled with the passion of different causes—Civil Rights, Vietnam, Berkeley, the environment among them—with the fringes peopled by the extremists. The so-called Counter Culture had run to excesses (from the traditional view) in music, dance, fashion, drugs, general life style, while the "me" generation ('doing my own thing') seemed to celebrate individuality at the expense of institutional support and loyalty. The Judge was especially interested in the relevance of wise restraints in the balancing of individual liberty with societal well-being. It was not a problem just for the courts but for "all of us in formulating and expressing our political and social philosophies."

Wise restraints suggested a sense of perspective as the means of expressing dissent and effecting necessary social reforms. He quoted Senator Edmund Muskie of Maine in cautioning against undue patience. "To argue for some tolerance of delay in the correction of apparent wrong is not to plead against conscience...it is a reminder that democracy chokes on too many non-negotiable demands. If every wrong demands a holy crusade, we shall have many crusades but little peace and less freedom."[14] Patience and openness to both sides of controversial questions are essential for those who would reform society. As Oliver Wendell Holmes once suggested, rather than "sweeping away all opposition," the "ultimate good desired is better reached by free trade in ideas..."[15]

In any event, the cause does not justify violence and lawlessness in pressing for reform. Peaceful and lawful dissent and protest are clearly protected by the First Amendment and must be respected, defended, and even encouraged. By contrast, what is called civil disobedience "is the deliberate and open violation of any law which an individual or group believes to be unjust with a view toward effecting its change, or the commission of a similar unlawful act in order to influence government policy."[16] In the words of Earl Morris, a past president of the A.B.A., what "is reprehensible in these acts is not the point of view, not the end to be achieved—one may or may not agree with them—but the method of achieving them."[17]

One justifiable type of civil disobedience, he noted again as he had done so often in speeches, involved the testing in court of the constitutionality of a particular law. That might involve violating the questionable statute. In that event, if the trial court finds the law valid, the person who has violated it must be prepared to take the legal consequences. So, in the field of civil rights, he felt that the violation of many statutes in Southern states had been justified in order to determine the constitutionality of the acts. But when a law has been found valid, he could not justify further violation.

One consequence of civil disobedience, evident in the times, is the tendency to condone a general disrespect for law and to suggest that "each citizen has a right to determine for himself which laws are just and which laws should be obeyed." As a member of the President's Crime Commission had pointed out, "One of the most appalling and frightening of the trends in recent years is the self-serving practice of choosing which laws or court orders to obey and which to defy.... To rest upon or hide behind the claim that if one's conscience speaks to the contrary, justification exists for ignoring laws or decrees is but to say that the rule of law is not to be the governing yardstick of our society's conduct."[18]

Also, implicit in civil disobedience is the very real danger of escalation, that unlawful but peaceful protest may get out of hand and lead to mob violence. Such a danger, he recalled, had been eloquently articulated by Mr. Justice Black: "Experience demonstrates that it is not a far step from what to many seems the earnest, honest, patriotic, kind-spirited multitude of today, to the fanatical, threatening, lawless mob of tomorrow. And the crowds that press in the streets for noble goals today can be supplanted tomorrow by street mobs pressuring...for precisely opposite ends."[19] The final result of such violence is to breed counter-violence, backlash, repressive measures, and the loss of freedom. Wise restraints on excesses, practiced by every citizen, are needed to keep us free. Or, as President Eisenhower once remarked, "Liberty is the priceless opportunity for self-discipline."

Then the following year he was at Gonzaga's 83rd Commencement to receive the University Law Medal. Toward the end of the decade (November 16, 1979), with many speeches in between, the Judge rode over to the School of Law to deliver the Second Blankenbaker Lecture on Professional Responsibility. His particular topic was "The Bench, The Bar, and the Press." Missoula, of course, was like a second home and the place of repeated honors. In 1972 he had received the UM Alumni Association's Distinguished Service Award. A lifetime member of Phi Delta Phi (legal fraternity), he had had a new Barrister's Inn named for him at the Law School in 1978. His ties with the School went back over 60 years—to the fall of 1919 when he had entered a still new institution. He had helped to dedicate the new Law Building in 1961 on the School's 50th Anniversary and in June 1979 had given the keynote address in ceremonies for the new wing. For years he had served on the Board of Visitors, so his ties were close indeed.

The Judge was proud of his alma mater for being one of the first law schools in the country to offer a separate and required course in professional responsibility. He noted with approval that in 1974 the A.B.A. had amended the standards for the approval of law schools to include a provision requiring the law school to "provide and require. . .for a professional degree, instruction in the duties and responsibilities of the legal profession. . . .Each law school is encouraged to involve members of the bench and bar in such instruction."[20] It was fortunate that the Blankenbaker Foundation was providing an annual endowment to the Law School to supplement its program in professional responsibility.

With regard to the bench, the Judge found the court's responsibilities complicated by an increasingly complex society. The high tribunal, especially, is constantly reconciling and balancing conflicting viewpoints—"balancing the different rights guaranteed by the Constitution of the United States, particulary under the First, Fourth, Fifth and Sixth Amendments;. . .balancing those rights with acts of Congress and regulatory bodies;. . .balancing the rights of the federal and state governments; and in some of our Indian cases balancing treaty rights with Acts of Congress and rights of the state." In view of this perennial problem, it is understandable why the courts "reach different conclusions and why there are so many differing opinions among justices of the Supreme Court on some of the most controversial issues."[21]

Yet, too often, the Supreme Court in particular is caught in a sharp crossfire of those who feel it has become too "imperial," upsurping powers not granted by the Constitution, and those who criticize it as being too timid in not engaging in "social and political activism" required by society's needs. In surveying current criticisms of the Court, the Judge discussed cases involving actions of libel, the right of the press to withhold information pertinent to criminal prosecution,and the right of the press to gain access to information.

With regard to the bar, the Judge felt strongly that lawyers have a special responsibility to the public. In a particular way, their role as officers of the court carries with it the broader responsibilities of citizenship. He agreed with his long-time friend, Mr. Justice Powell, that in "a democracy there is always a need for leadership, and throughout our history lawyers have been expected to provide it. Alexis de Tocqueville, nearly a century and a half ago, questioned 'whether democratic institutions could long be maintained. . .if the influence of lawyers in public business did not increase in proportion to the power of the people.' "[22]

In the Judge's view, lawyers have a special duty to seek elective office, "to serve on public boards and commissions, and to participate in civic, charitable and cultural organizations in their community." Generally, he felt that Montana lawyers had accepted those kinds of responsibility. However, he wondered about their declining interest in state government. "My feeling is that our system of justice would be enchanced and the needs of some of our institutions better recognized if we had more lawyers, and particularly graduates of the University of Montana Law School, in our state legislature."

The press, of course, has a critical role in modern society, to bring the citizenry the facts on the operation of government. "Great responsibility is...placed upon the news media to accurately and fairly report judicial proceedings to guarantee the fairness of the trial and to bring to bear the beneficial effects of public scrutiny upon the administration of justice." He noted that while "the First Amendment has not created any special privilege for the press apart from that available for the public...additional privileges may be created by legislation and court rules, provided the exercise of the privilege does not prejudice the right of an accused to a fair trial."

The Judge also noted that the newsman's privilege to keep the sources of information confidential "does not extend to withholding from the court relevant information which may be necessary to protect constitutional rights of others to a fair trial." In conclusion, he stated that "the court, bar and press alike owe a duty to the public to promote truth and justice, to act fairly, and to report accurately—an obligation which is becoming increasingly important in our complex society. There is a compelling need today for all of us to cooperate in insuring the fairness of trials and promoting and enhancing the administration of justice."

V.

As the Judge crossed over his 20th and 25th anniversaries on the federal bench, grateful colleagues in the law gathered at the federal courtroom in Billings to celebrate an unusually notable career. There were telegrams from the Chief Justice and Associate Justices like Lewis F. Powell, Jr., with whom he had shared so many assignments since their first meeting at Canyon in Yellowstone Park back in 1952. There were greetings from Judges Lumbard and Tamm and others with whom he had sat on the circuit courts. There were commendations from the Montana Supreme Court and a proclamation by Billings' mayor designating April 2, 1982, as "W. J. Jameson Day." There were also, very importantly, the testimonials of law clerks from across the years as to what he had meant to them as they stood at the threshold of their careers. They spoke of his forceful intelligence, integrity, patience, and kindness. They were grateful for the legacy of honesty, fairness, and compassion which was shared by all whose lives he had touched.

When he had retired from the active judgeship, his old friend of National Defender days, General Charles Decker, had written that "there must be a source of personal inspiration for each man who scales the heights, and therefore a tribute to Mrs. Jameson, always at his side, is most fitting on this occasion."[23] Numerous speakers on the anniversary programs underscored that sentiment. The Montana Supreme Court extended "congratulations not only to Judge Jameson, but also to his faithful wife who has been a part of his activities for these many years."

Mildred made that decision from the very beginning and never looked back as they journeyed together with the law. As homemaker she relieved her husband of the minor distractions of daily life so that he could concentrate on his work. Fortunately, she was able to be a frequent companion in his travels, especially after the children were grown. Whenever the destination made driving possible, she was both at the wheel and navigator, giving him time to prepare for his meeting. She was able to share in the widening circle of friendship, adding her own gifts of personality, as he made his way to the top of his profession. The university English major also read the first draft of his speeches, correcting grammar where indicated. If she was his most ardent supporter, she was also his most devoted critic! She regularly perused his professional literature, claiming that she actually read more law journals than he had time to do.

But there were spaces in their togetherness and Mildred maintained her own independence and integrity. Her early activities had included the American Association of Univeristy Women, which she served one year as president. The AAUP was the city's first study group, initially investigating the secrets of child care

Mrs. W.J. Jameson playing Christmas music to Deaconess Hospital patients

Fiftieth Wedding Anniversary, 1973

before moving on to Russian History. Music remained a major outlet, from the time she played at the Presbyterian, Baptist, and Congregational Churches before moving to the Methodist Church for a twenty-five year stay! At Christmas she played her organ in the hallways of Deaconess Hospital to bring a bit of Yuletide cheer. She was a strong supporter of the Billings Symphony and the Community Concert Association and, when traveling to meetings, tried to attend a musical or an opera.

For thirty years Mildred was active in the Girl Scouts, starting with Mary Lucille and continuing with granddaughter Liz. She served as a commissioner during World War II, and that was when she injured her back collecting and carting grease to earn money for the Twin Pines Camp on the rims. She always figured that she deserved the Purple Heart! Hobbies and interests across the years included reading (especially history and historical novels), gardening, bird watching, and cooking. She specialized in holiday dinners as a way of getting all the family together in the home. She was an enthusiastic spectator at sports events and a loyal fan of the T.V. program "MASH".[24]

Mildred had begun attending the A.B.A. meetings with Bill in 1937 and did not miss more than two or three in all. Looking back over the years, she would feel lucky that he had wanted to include her. Young lawyers' wives, she reflected, should at least take a positive attitude toward their husbands' work. Part of her compensation had been the interesting people and the memorable

Sixtieth Wedding Anniversary Reception

times—like Boston in 1953, Chicago in 1954, the London visit and meeting the Queen Mother, and the awarding of the A.B.A. gold medal in Washington. She had found watching "tough sessions" of the House of Delegates rather fascinating when issues like electronic surveillance were on the table. Her husband and other past presidents like Lewis Powell had a way of "swinging things".

"They were real operators, virtually unbeatable," she recalled with a smile.

On July 28, 1973 the Jamesons celebrated their 50th Wedding Anniversary. It was one of those beautiful, sunny, relaxed days of summer at Camp Senia with a few of their old time friends and all of the children and grandchildren except Kathy. She couldn't get away from her job as musical director at the Bigfork Summer Playhouse. The day had an added pleasure when Liz announced her wedding in December. Ten years later Bill and Mildred observed their 60th Anniversary with many friends attending a reception at Brother Van Hall in the Methodist Church.

The new year brought health problems for Mildred and on January 16th she was admitted to Deaconess Hospital. She died on February 4, 1984. Her passing meant the pain of loss such as only those can know who have shared a close companionship with common values and aspirations. Yet, death is tragic only where there has been no nurturing of meaning, no victories of the human spirit, signifying a life well lived. She knew how to share the gifts of time and caring with the young lives of Girl Scouts and the frail lives of the ill and elderly, to brighten their days with her friendship and her music. She had had the deep and enduring satisfactions of a happy marriage with children and their children to cherish and enjoy. She had savored the fruits of hard work rewarded, of the dedication she and her husband had brought to his profession. Waste no sadness on the Mildred Jamesons of this life, for they have known the joy of believing in a cause worth serving in a world in which they have been truly at home.

EPILOGUE

The Judge's journey with the law remains unfinished. He has been again to Missoula—for the 31st law clerk since 1957. On his desk and conference table lies the evidence of a jurist very much at work. As these lines are written, he is preparing to attend another A.B.A. Annual Meeting in Chicago. President Wallace D. Riley has invited him to be on the platform for the dedication of a new and enlarged Bar headquarters at Northwestern University Law School. The American Bar Center of 1954 has been outgrown by an Association membership surpassing 290,000. He is the oldest living A.B.A. president in point of service (also of the Montana Bar and the American Judicature Society), so the ranks are thinning of those who have fought with him the good fight for a better administration of justice in the land. Yet, there will be enough to greet their esteemed colleague from Montana and to share memories of their several sojourns with the law.

It has been 62 years since he was admitted to the Montana Bar and started his practice of law. It has been 60 years since he was elected secretary of the M.B.A. and began his interest in bar related activities. He remembers the meeting of the Montana Bar in 1925 when the major theme was "Proposed Reforms for Judicial and Administrative Proceedings." Judge George B. Winston was one of the speakers and quoted Chief Justice Taft that we had "fallen furtherest from our ideal conditions in our whole government" in "our failure to secure expedition and thoroughness in the enforcement of public and private rights in the courts." In his conclusion, Winston emphasized that every member of the bar "should realize that he owes a service to society other than . . . that of just being a lawyer." Seldom have the urgings of a speaker found more fruitful expression than they did in the heart and mind and labors of the young attorney from Billings.

As the Judge reflects on the past, he thinks first of those who have helped to make his career with the bar possible, of his partners and associates during 35 years of practice who approved of his participation and relieved him of many office duties. He has been fortunate in having a cooperative family, including a very supportive sister. During his 27 years on the court, there have been three very dedicated and efficient secretaries and thirty law clerks who have assisted in his extra-judicial but bar related activities. He notes with satisfaction that many of the law clerks have later assumed active roles in various bar organizations. Above all, he has been most fortunate in having a sympathetic and understanding wife, who for 60 years had shared the burdens, the responsibilities, and the great rewards of their bar association work.

In appraising the achievements and failures of the law during the past 60 years, he feels that it is important to keep in mind Justice Powell's admonition that we must balance "the frustrations of how far we have to go" with the satisfaction of how far we have come. While much remains to be done, the Judge thinks "we can still take pride in the significant role played by the organized bar in the recognition of Civil Rights, in fighting discrimination, in recruiting lawyers from minority groups, in providing legal aid for those unable to pay for services, in providing representation for indigent persons accused of crime, in recognizing the rights of the mentally ill, and most recently in encouraging proper recognition of the rights of victims of crime."

He takes particular satisfaction in his participation in five incidents which illustrate the progress that has been made during the past 60 years. First was the removal of any racial restrictions in membership in the American Bar Association. Second was the progress in providing legal services for the poor. Third was the adoption by the American Bar Association in 1951 of the recommendation of the Committee on Scope and Correlation of Work (which he chaired) of the six long-range objectives of the Association. Fourth was the adoption, following the Army-McCarthy controversy, of the report of the A.B.A. Committee on Individual Rights and National Security, proposing rules of procedure for Congressional investigations. Finally, there was the privilege of serving as chairman of the very important A.B.A. Committee for the Administration of Criminal Justice.

As the Judge surveys the contemporary scene, he notes that many "persons feel that there is a tendency today to place undue emphasis on the rights of those charged with or convicted of crime, and to fail to recognize the rights of society and victims of crime. In other words, we sometimes overlook the admonition of Justice Cardoza that 'Justice, though due the accused, is due the accuser also,' that we 'must keep the balance true.' Many feel that we have gone too far in post conviction remedies through excessive and repetitious appeals and in permitting defendants who are obviously guilty go free by excluding so-called tainted evidence."[1]

The Judge predicts a stricter application of Justice Powell's statement that "the ultimate question of guilt or innocence" should be "the central concern of a criminal proceeding." 'This," he feels, "should result in a wider recognition of finality in criminal judgments and a rejection, except in rare instances, of review by federal courts of state court convictions where there has been a full and fair litigation of a defendant's constitutional rights. It should also avoid post conviction proceedings where a case has been fully and fairly litigated prior to judgment. It may well result in a modification of the exclusionary rule to avoid *per se* exclusion of questionable evidence and give the trial judge more discretion—permitting consideration of the nature and substantiality of the violation by the arresting officer and whether he acted in good faith, recognizing the role of proportionality that is essential to the concept of justice."[2]

The Judge looks for greater citizen participation in detecting and preventing crime, as he also believes that the "litigation explosion" will necessitate more nonjudicial kinds of resolution of many disputes. Such alternative means may involve small claims courts, legal services offices, governmental agencies, local social agencies, and various types of arbitration, conciliation and mediation services.

At the heart of his outlook upon the law and life is the concept of the "balanced perspective." He expounded it around the country during his year as A.B.A. president and has been guided by its wisdom during his tenure on the bench. "In maintaining the freedom we enjoy," he observes, "perhaps our greatest need today is to keep a proper balance and a proper perspective of history in formulating and expressing our political and social philosophies. I don't presume there has ever been a time in the history of our country when it has been more important and necessary that we avoid the pressures of extremists and strive for a balanced viewpoint in the solution of our many complex problems. The extremists on either side are rarely the guardians of human freedom. Too often we fail to recognize that there are two sides to controversial questions. The late Learned Hand, one of the outstanding jurists of our time, once said that, 'The Spirit of Liberty is the spirit which is not too sure it is right.' It is important also, whether we regard ourselves as conservatives, liberals, or moderates that our position is not determined by whose ox is being gored."

"There is a desperate need today," the Judge concludes, "for the spirit of compromise, goodwill, and balancing conflicting viewpoints which guided the fathers of our country. We must balance our obligations as a world power with a realistic appraisal of our capabilities and self interest. We must balance the need for expanded energy with the protection of our environment; the need to keep government expenditures within reason and still provide needed services. We must balance the right of privacy with the public's right to know, and personal freedom with public safety. We must balance the protection and rights of society and the victims of crime with the rights of the accused. Finally, we must keep a proper perspective in balancing the accomplishments of the past with the frustrations of the present and our hope for the future."

The goal of the balanced perspective is justice which, as Webster said, "is the greatest interest of man on Earth." Our capacity for justice makes the quest possible, but our proneness to injustice makes the quest necessary. Granted the human condition, justice is more a destination than a secured abiding place. It remains more a star at the edge of the night. It is the redeeming thought that every human being is a child of the Creator, entitled to fairness and the opportunity to find his or her way. So the Judge has fretted over the future of the young Indian brought before him. So he has pursued the well-being of life's unfortunates with a deep, humanitarian caring.

The "country lawyer" is how he once described himself, but the years summoned him to walk in high places and help to shape the legal destinies of the land. In a very real way, the journey had begun in the long thoughts of the small boy watching the judges come and go in his childhood town. Later, as a high school junior, he had discerned the trailmarks—diligent study of the statutes, integrity in the face of many temptations, courage to bear the disappointments, humility and humanitarian caring to keep first things first. The thoughts of that distant yesterday have been confirmed by a career which will be valued and remembered by all those whose lives it has touched.

RESEARCH NOTES

Much of the material for this publication has come from the private papers of the William J. Jameson Family, from diaries, recollections, correspondence, scrapbook memorabilia, unpublished speeches, and miscellaneous papers. In addition, several interviews with Judge and Mrs. Jameson, daughter Mary and son Bill, Jr., have provided important insights, interesting stories, and a proper perspective for the narrative. It was especially helpful to have available Will Jameson's diary for the late 1880's and Lucille Jameson Armsby's detailed and extended recollection of the family background and early years. Another prinicipal source of information has been the local newspapers, especially in the Judge's home towns, along with publications of the American Bar Association and related bar organizations.

Chapter One. **Heritage**

1. *Correspondence.* Lucille Jameson Armsby to William J. Jameson, July 26, 1977. This 27 page, single-spaced letter contains much valuable data on the Jameson family. Correspondence addressed to "My Brother and Cousins," dated August 20, 1971 and August 3, 1977 provides additional interesting information. This source will appear as *Correspondence* below.

2. *Montana Standard* (date unavailable), Butte folio, Vertical File, Montana Room, Parmly Billings Library.

3. *Montana Standard,* June 5, 1949.

4. "Word Picture of Butte in 1889 as Seen by Eastern Newswriter," Butte folio, Vertical File, Montana Room, Parmly Billings Library.

5. *Will Jameson's Diary,* April 25, 1886.

6. Michael P. Malone, *The Battle for Butte, Mining and Politics on the Northern Frontier, 1864-1906,* University of Washington, 1981. Chapter 4 on "Boom Town" contains interesting background information.

7. See Lawrence F. Small, *A Century of Politics on the Yellowstone,* Billings, 1983, 39.

8. *Helena Daily Herald,* November 8, 1889.

9. *Correspondence,* 5.

10. *Correspondence,,* 11.

Chapter Two. **Childhood**

1. *Thirteenth Census of the United States 1910. Abstract Supplement for Montana 579, 580.*

2. *The Butte Miner,* Dec. 17, 1897.

3. *The Butte Miner,* Jan. 1, 1898, p. 4, (first column under The New Year).

4. *The Butte Miner,* Dec. 1897-Jan. 1898 has frequent references to the gambling issue.

5. *Correspondence,* 13.

6. *Montana Standard,* August 11, 1957.

7. Betty Wetzel, "Coming Home," *Montana Magazine,* July-August, 1983, 60.

8. William J. Jameson, Jr., "Law," English III, October 20, 1913.

Chapter Three. **Preparations and Beginnings**

1. *Missoula, The Garden City,* (pamphlet), Chamber of Commerce, Missoula, Montana, 1910, 2.

2. Harold G. Merriam, *The University of Montana, A History,* University of Montana Press, 1970, 2.

3. Merriam, 3.

4. Merriam, viii.

5. Inverview with Merle C. Gallagher, Feb. 15, 1984.

6. *Correspondence,* 23.

7. Merriam, 54.

8. Merriam, 26, 27.

9. Merriam, 80.
10. William J. Jameson, Lecture, Rocky Mountain College, March 16, 1978, 5.

Chapter Four. **The Widening Way**

1. *Billings Gazette and Evening Journal,* Anniversary Edition, 1914, article by James R. Goss.
2. Harley Henderson and Lawrence F. Small, *Montana Passage, A Homesteader's Heritage,* Billings, 1983, 65.
3. *The Billings Gazette,* November 18, 1928.
4. Chapter 6, 1927 *Session Laws.*
5. Clark C. Spence, *Montana, A History,* Norton & Co. Inc.,, New York, 1978, 143.
6. William J. Jameson, "Lincoln's Birthday Address, 1929," Montana Legislature.
7. William J. Jameson, "Charter Day Address, 1930," University of Montana.
8. *The Billings Gazette,,* June 13, 193l.
9. *The Billings Gazette,* Sunday, May 22, 1927.
10. Ellis Waldron and Paul B. Wilson, *Atlas of Montana Elections 1889-1976, University of Montana, 1978, 135.*
11. William J. Jameson,*"The Development and Significance of Our Service Clubs," 1924.*

Chapter Five. **Road to the A.B.A.**

1. *Proceedings of the Montana Bar Association,* 1937—1941, 107.
2. American Bar Foundation Program on Oral History; Transcript of Interview with William J. Jameson; Olavi Maru, interviewer, June 17, 1975.
3. *Proceedings,* 95.
4. William J. Jameson, Unpublished lecture at Rocky Mountain College, March 25, 1980.
5. Burton K. Wheeler (with Paul F. Healy), *Yankee from the West,* N.Y. 1962, Doubleday, Garden City, N.Y. 331, 335.
6. Jameson lecture at R.M.C.
7. Willis Van Devanter, Unpublished speech.
8. *Proceedings,* 106.
9. *Proceedings,* 96.
10. *Proceedings,* 104.
11. Transcript of Jameson interview with Olavi Maru.
12. *Yellowstone News,* February 26, 1953.
13. *Yellowstone News,* February 26, 1953.

14. Correspondence with Michael F. Lamb, May 29, 1984.
15. *Great Falls Tribune*, "Montana Parade," August 16, 1959. See also *The Daily Missoulian*, January 15, 1957, for an editorial on Judge Pray's career.
16. *Great Falls Tribune*, "Montana Parade," August 16, 1959.
17. Jameson lecture at R.M.C.
18. Jameson lecture at R.M.C.
19. *The Daily Missoulian*, January 20, 1942.
20. *Montana Standard*, March 17, 1944.
21. William J. Jameson, "Future Program of Billings Commercial Club."
22. *A.B.A. Daily Bar Bulletin*, September, 1951.
23. *The Yellowstone News*, June 26, 1952.
24. *The Daily Missoulian*, January 16, 1953.

Chapter Six. **At the Summit**

1. *Billings Times*, December 15, 1953.
2. *New York Times*, May 20, 1953.
3. *Yellowstone News*, August 11, 1953.
4. American Bar Foundation Program on Oral History; Transcript of Interview with William J. Jameson; Olavi Maru, Interviewer, Billings, June 17, 1975.
5. William J. Jameson, "Balancing Individual Rights with National Security," September 14, 1953.
6. *Yellowstone News*, clipping (date unavailable), Jameson Papers
7. Unpublished correspondence.
8. *American Bar Association Journal*, September 1953, 793.
9. William J. Jameson, "Balancing Individual Rights with National Security," September 14, 1953.
10. *Minneapolis Sunday Times*, December 6, 1953.
11. *Los Angeles Times*, January 22, 1954.
12. Family file clipping, date not noted.
13. *American Bar Association Journal*, May 1954, 356.
14. *The Daily Missoulian*, May 11, 1954.
15. *Oregon Journal*, Portland, May 15, 1954.
16. William J. Jameson, "Service to the Public and Legal Profession—A Reappraisal," Annual Address, August 16, 1954.
17. *American Bar Association Journal*, October 1954, 835.
18. *Chicago Daily Tribune*, August 18, 1954.
19. *Chicago Daily Tribune*, August 17, 1954.
20. *American Bar Association Journal*, October 1954, 835.

21. *Chicago Daily Tribune,* August 20, 1954.

Chapter Seven. **Judge Jameson**

1. "Ceremony Honoring the Honorable William J. Jameson on the occasion of his Twentieth year on the Federal Bench (1957-1977), April 22, 1977," Federal Building, Billings, Montana, remarks by J. Martin Burke, 32, 33.
2. *The Daily Missoulian, October 24, 1954.*
3. *American Bar News,* December 15, 1956.
4. *Great Falls Tribune,* January 22, 1957.
5. *Great Falls Tribune,* March 6, 1957.
6. *The Daily Missoulian,* March 6, 1957.
7. *Great Falls Tribune,* April 11, 1957.
8. *The Helena Independent,* June 16, 1957.
9. *Great Falls Tribune,* May 17, 1957.
10. "Response of William J. Jameson at Dinner to American Bar Association Members in the Middle Temple, July 27, 1957" (unpublished address).
11. Frank E. Holman, *London Revisited* (pamphlet), October 1957, 28.
12. *The Christian Science Monitor,* August 8, 1957.
13. Holman, 32.
14. Kathryn Wright, interview, *The Billings Gazette,* August 25, 1957.
15. "Ceremony honoring the Honorable William J. Jameson, etc.," remarks by Sam Haddon, 30.
16. "Ceremony" remarks by J. Martin Burke, 33.
17. Burke, 34, 35.
18. *Fortune, December, 1961, 91.*
19. *"Ceremony," remarks by Bruce C. Toole.*
20. *The Daily Missoulian,* August 29, 1959.
21. William J. Jameson, "The National Judicial College," unpublished papers.
22. William J. Jameson, "The National Defender Project," unpublished papers.
23. William J. Jameson, "Progress in Montana," *The Legal Aid Briefcase,* February, 1968, 140.
24. Jameson, "Progress in Montana," 141-2.
25. *Correspondence,* Charles L. Decker to Frank A. Gallagher, June 6, 1969.
26. *Electing the President, A Report on the Commission on Elec-*

toral College Reform, (pamphlet), American Bar Association, January, 1967, vii.
27. *Electing the President,* 37.
28. *The Western Political Quarterly,* September, 1958, 714.
29. *The Western Political Quarterly,* September, 1958, 720.
30. *The Western Political Quarterly,* September, 1958, 721.
31. *The Daily Missoulian,* June 2, 1963.
32. William J. Jameson, "Civil Disobedience and the Right of Dissent," unpublished address before the Billings Rotary Club, December 30, 1968.
33. *The Billings Gazette,* February 20, 1969.

Chapter Eight. **The Senior Circuit**
1. *The Billings Gazette,* June 12, 1969.
2. *The Daily Missoulian,* November 24, 1971.
3. William J. Jameson, unpublished papers.
4. *The Daily Missoulian,* August 16, 1974.
5. *The Independent Record,* Helena, June 15, 1978, article by John Willard.
6. William J. Jameson, "The Iranian Cases," unpublished papers.
7. *Chicago Daily Tribune,* August 17, 1954.
8. William J. Jameson, "The Background and Development of the Criminal Justice Standards," *Judicature,* May 1972, 367.
9. William J. Jameson, "Presentation of Second Edition of ABA Standards of Criminal Justice to Supreme Court of Montana," October 27, 1980.
10. *Washington Star,* undated clipping (February, 1971) in family papers.
11. *American Bar News,* October, 1973.
12. *The Billings Gazette,* May 17, 1974.
13. *Correspondence* with Brent R. Cromley, April 12, 1984.
14. William J. Jameson, "Those Wise Restraints Which make Men Free," Founders Day Address, Rocky Mountain College, May 31, 1969, 7.
15. "Those Wise Restraints," 8.
16. "Those Wise Restraints," 10.
17. "Those Wise Restraints," 10.
18. "Those Wise Restraints," 13, 14.
19. "Those Wise Restraints," 14.
20. William J. Jameson, "Blankenbaker Lecture," University of Montana Law School, November 17, 1979, 2.
21. "Blankenbaker Lecture," 4, 5.

22. "Blankenbaker Lecture," 40.
23. *Correspondence,* General Charles L. Decker to Frank A. Gallagher, June 6, 1969.
24. The Rev. Dr. Vern L. Klingman, Eulogy for Mildred Theone Lore Jameson, February 7, 1984.

Epilogue

1, 2. William J. Jameson, "Administration of Justice," unpublished paper.

INDEX

ABOUT THE AUTHOR

Lawrence F. Small is a native of Maine where he received undergraduate and graduate degrees at the University of Maine, a divinity degree from Bangor Theological Seminary, and the Ph.D. in History from Harvard University. Following pastorates in Massachusetts and New Jersey, he went to Rocky Mountain College in Billings, Montana, in 1959, where he has served on the faculty and as dean and president. He has been Professor of History and Political Science since 1975. His publications include two books, *Montana Passage, A Homesteader's Heritage* (with Harley Henderson) and *A Century of Politics On The Yellowstone.*

He is married and the father of four children, all living in Montana.